Bob Bergland

Experience God in Worship

Perspectives on the future of worship in the church from today's most prominent worship leaders including

GEORGE BARNA, GARY M. BURGE, RICHARD ALLEN FARMER, LISA HARPER, JACK W. HAYFORD, KIM HILL, BRUCE H. LEAFBLAD, JOHN S. MILLER, LEONARD SWEET, and ROBERT WEBBER

Group

Loveland, Colorado

Experience God in Worship

Copyright © 2000 Group Publishing, Inc.

Visit our Web site: **www.grouppublishing.com**

Credits
Editor: Michael D. Warden
Creative Development Editor: Jim Kochenburger
Chief Creative Officer: Joani Schultz
Contributing Writer: Dennis McLaughlin
Copy Editor: Janis Sampson
Art Director: Kari K. Monson
Computer Graphic Artist: Pat Miller
Cover Art Director: Jeff A. Storm
Cover Designer: Alan Furst, Inc.
Production Manager: Alexander Jorgensen

Library of Congress Cataloging-in-Publication Data

Experience God in worship : perspectives on the future of worship in the church from today's most prominent leaders/including George Barna... [et al.].
     p. cm.
   ISBN 0-7644-2133-6
    1. Public worship. I. Barna, George.
   BV15 .E87 2000
   264'.001'12--dc21   99-042148

10 9 8 7 6 5 4 3 2 1   09 08 07 06 05 04 03 02 01 00

Printed in the United States of America.

About the Authors

GEORGE BARNA is the president of Barna Research Group, Ltd., a marketing research company located in Ventura, California. The company specializes in conducting primary research for Christian ministries and nonprofit organizations. Since its inception in 1984, Barna Research has served more than two hundred ministries and other nonprofit organizations. George Barna has written more than twenty books including *The Frog in the Kettle, User Friendly Churches, The Power of Vision,* and *Evangelism That Works.* His most recent book is titled *The Second Coming of the Church.* He lives with his wife, Nancy, and their two daughters, Samantha and Corban, in Southern California.

DR. GARY M. BURGE is Professor of New Testament at Wheaton College and Graduate School (Wheaton, Illinois). He is a graduate of the University of California; Fuller Theological Seminary; King's College; and the University of Aberdeen (Scotland), where he earned his Ph.D. in New Testament. In addition to a variety of articles, he has published extensively on the writings of John. His most recent commentary is *The NIV Application Commentary on the Letters of John.* Its companion volume, *The NIV Application Commentary on the Gospel of John,* is also now available.

DR. RICHARD ALLEN FARMER is a Bible expositor and concert artist. He holds a Bachelor of Music degree from Nyack College, Nyack, New York; a Master of Divinity degree from Princeton Theological Seminary, Princeton, New Jersey; and honorary doctorates from both Gordon and Houghton colleges in the state of New York. A compelling preacher, pianist, and vocalist, Farmer has preached and given concerts in most major U.S. cities and at several mission stations throughout the world. He and his wife, Rosemary, and son, Timothy, make their home in Dallas, Texas.

LISA HARPER, co-writer with Kim Hill, is the creator of Renewing the Heart, a national Christian women's conference sponsored by Focus on the Family. She recently co-authored two books, *Renewed Hearts, Changed Lives* and *May Bell's Daughter*. She was executive producer of *Renewing the Heart Live* worship project, which won a Dove Award. She speaks at women's events around the country and works at Christ Presbyterian Church in Nashville, Tennessee.

DR. JACK W. HAYFORD is the senior pastor of the ten-thousand-member congregation of The Church on the Way located in Van Nuys, California. He is a graduate of LIFE Bible College and Azusa Pacific University and holds three honorary doctorates. Hayford founded both The King's College and The King's Seminary located in Los Angeles. He hosts the national television and international radio program *Living Way* and has written almost three dozen books including *Worship His Majesty* and *Moments With Majesty*. Hayford has composed over five hundred songs, choruses, and hymns; his most noted is the classic "Majesty."

KIM HILL has recorded six albums with nine number-one singles and has received both a Grammy Award nomination and a Dove Award. Currently, she serves as worship leader for Focus on the Family's Renewing the Heart conferences, which attract ten to twenty thousand women to each event. Her deepest desire is to worship through her music and in her daily routine as a wife and mother. She strives to "glorify God and to enjoy his presence."

DR. BRUCE H. LEAFBLAD is Professor of Church Music and Worship and Fellow of the Scarborough Institute for Church Growth at Southwestern Baptist Theological Seminary in Fort Worth, Texas. In addition to teaching at Bethel College and Seminary in St. Paul, he has been an adjunct or guest professor at Fuller Seminary, Talbot Seminary, and seminaries in Canada, South Korea, and the Philippines. Leafblad has conducted more than twenty worship conferences a year for nearly two decades and has been a frequent contributor to books, journals, and magazines. For ten years he served as minister of music and worship at Lake Avenue Church in Pasadena, California. He and his wife, June, live in Fort Worth and have two married children, Stewart and Stefani.

JOHN S. MILLER, worship pastor of The Next Level Church, is being used by God to inspire and lead a new generation of worshippers. With a heart for innovative and relevant means of worship, Miller has opened the door to a new depth of worship for the people of The Next Level Church and for others across the country. Through leading worship, writing songs, and teaching the values of worship, Miller is active in restoring his generation to becoming authentic worshippers of God. He holds a Bachelor of Science degree in Music Engineering from the University of Colorado at Denver.

DR. LEONARD SWEET is widely known on three fronts: as a historian of American culture, as a semiotician who "reads" postmodern culture, and as a preacher to a postmodern age who bridges the worlds of academe and popular culture. Currently he is dean of the Theological School, vice president, and professor of postmodern Christianity at Drew University in Madison, New Jersey. Author of more than one hundred articles, over four hundred published sermons, and fourteen books, Sweet has been the writer for the past eight years of *Homiletics,* the premier preaching resource in North America. His most recent books include *AquaChurch, Eleven Genetic Gateways to Spiritual Awakening, A Cup of Coffee at the Soul Cafe,* and *SoulTsunami.*

DR. ROBERT WEBBER is recognized by pastors, denominational leaders, and scholars as one of the foremost authorities on worship renewal. Webber is the director of the Institute for Worship Studies, professor of theology at Wheaton College, and affiliate professor of worship at Northern Seminary in Lombard, Illinois. He has conducted workshops on the topic of worship with nearly every major Christian denomination, ministry, and fellowship in North America. He is the author of more than a dozen books including *Worship Old and New* and *Worship Is a Verb* and is the editor of the eight-volume work *The Complete Library of Christian Worship.*

Contents

Introduction

From the days of the tabernacle to the present, believers have been striving to give God glory in worship. The attempts to give God glory have taken on many different forms throughout the ages. *Experience God in Worship* presents "windows" into some of the most significant expressions of worship in North America at the beginning of the new millennium.

George Barna opens the window on worship with a perspective on worship in the third millennium. He cites much of his recent research to explain the challenges and problems facing church leaders called to facilitate worship in their congregations. Barna closes with the prayer "that we may exploit the inner yearning that millions possess to be intimately connected with their Father in heaven through genuine, authentic, consistent, purposeful, loving, and pleasing expressions of worship."

Dr. Robert Webber provides detailed examples of churches with blended worship. He predicts that "the worship of the twenty-first century isn't the traditional worship of the Booster, nor the contemporary worship of the Boomer and early Buster, but a convergence of worship traditions molded by the latter Busters and Millennials, who are soon to become the leaders of our churches."

Dr. Gary Burge shares his own pilgrimage from charismatic renewal and evangelical worship to more liturgical forms of worship. He offers multiple examples of colleagues and students who "are looking for worship that weds dignity and spontaneity, worship that is theologically informed and liturgically intentional."

Kim Hill and Lisa Harper deliver a fresh perspective on contemporary worship from their roles as leaders of the Renewing the Heart conference for women. The power of contemporary music to lift the name of God is clearly illustrated and explained.

Dr. Bruce Leafblad explores evangelical worship for the twenty-first century. He details a biblical model for worship and closes by predicting that "a major aspect of worship renewal in the twenty-first century will focus on the recovery of biblical norms in worship, the restoration of biblical elements to worship, and the realignment of worship with biblical models and paradigms."

Dr. Richard Allen Farmer paints a picture of his own experiences of worship in the black church. He encourages churches from many traditions to learn the following lessons from the African-American tradition: "take your time, see your pastor differently, and let the people sing."

Dr. Jack Hayford offers David and Michal as case studies of biblical worship renewal. He exhorts the church to embrace expressive forms of worship in order to continue the contemporary reformation in worship that has sprung out of the charismatic movement. He states, "Worship that is spirit-filled provides insurance against simply learning facts from the Bible instead of receiving power through its teaching."

John Miller explains the importance of Gen-X worship from his platform as a worship pastor "to Gen Xers by Gen Xers." He envisions a day when a Gen-X "service will be a mixture of multiple elements being presented simultaneously for the congregation. During worship we might have a band playing; computer-generated slides with texts, Scriptures, and images; video; artwork; drama; dance; and poetry available in printed form or spoken as a time of meditation."

Dr. Leonard Sweet closes with an examination of worship in a post-modern world. He finds the pulse strongest in those churches which "transition their worship into more EPIC directions—Experiential, Participatory, Image-Based, and Communal."

This examination of multiple perspectives on worship on the eve of the new millennium was assembled with the prayerful desire to lift high the name of God and to celebrate the diverse forms of worship which are prominent in North America. May God use you in powerful new ways as you lead his people in worship.

Chapter 1
Worship in the Third Millennium

by GEORGE BARNA

There they were, the two superpowers, squaring off in neutral territory. Clearly having rehearsed this scene in eager anticipation of this occasion, Satan was going for broke. Here he was, one on one with God (in the form of Jesus Christ); it was show time, time to work his magic.

Satan initiated the competition with physical temptation, seeking to exploit Jesus' hunger and weakness, but to no avail. Undaunted, the evil one reassessed the situation and then struck again, testing Jesus' pride and security. But once again, he came up empty handed. Diligent to a fault, perhaps even sensing that God's Chosen One was tiring of these games, the devil knew it was time for the heavy artillery. Accordingly, he sought to be worshipped by the Son of God (Matthew 4:1-11).

But that pushed things too far. Satan quickly discovered that you can test God's patience, his power, and even his potential, but you simply can't toy with his heart. This has never been a secret. He was upfront with Moses and the Israelites about his limitations: He is a jealous God and will not allow intimacy with competing forces (Exodus 20:3-6). So as soon as Satan uttered the words "bow down and worship me," the contest was over. Surely it's no mistake that the first commandment is that we must not worship any other deity. Jesus himself reasserted the primacy of this demand when he described the Great Commandment—the necessity of pouring ourselves into a proper relationship with God and God alone (Matthew 22:34-40). This, Satan discovered, is one of the non-negotiables in God's universe.

For a nation that loves to cite its Christian allegiance—more than four out of five Americans describe themselves as "Christian"—we have an unimpressive record in the arena of worship.[1] Granted, virtually every Christian church in the nation provides at least one substantial opportunity for corporate worship every week. However, as I will describe in the pages that follow, we rarely worship God, whether we attend "worship services" or not. And how we respond to that reality may ultimately determine the fate of the nation, our churches, and their people.

America's Worship Problem

For the past several years we have found that adults consistently admit that even though they may regularly attend worship services at church, they rarely feel as if they connect with God during those events. To put some objective perspective to the state of worship in America, let's consider the following data from recent, nationwide surveys with large, representative samples of adults.

Failure to experience God's presence. Among adults who regularly attend church services, one-half admit that they haven't experienced God's presence at any time during the past year. Remember, this is not among the Easter-and-Christmas-only church attenders, but among people who attended an average of more than two dozen worship services last year.[2]

Responsibility to worship. Most adults will contend that a Christian has a responsibility to worship God. However, when asked to define what worship means, two out of three are unable to offer an appropriate definition or description of worship.

Even among the people who consistently attend Christian worship services, apparently for the purpose of worshipping God, the majority does not consider worship to be a "top priority" in their lives. It need not be the top priority; but most of them do not even include it among a laundry list of top priorities.[3]

> For most Americans worship is to satisfy or please them, not to honor or please God.

Reasons for worshipping. True to cultural form, the driving motivation behind the worship-event attendance of millions of adults is to have a pleasing experience. For most Americans worship is to satisfy or please them, not to honor or please God. Amazingly, few worship-service regulars argue that worship is something they do primarily for God; a substantially larger percentage of attenders claim that attending worship services is something that they do for personal benefit and pleasure.[4]

Quality of worship. "Good worship" is defined in numerous ways. Most people cite "good worship" as singing songs or hymns they like; hearing a sermon that we understand or rate favorably (either it is comforting, comfortable, or helpful); getting to interact with friends; or having successfully placated God through our voluntary attendance.[5]

Pastoral approaches to genuine worship. Amazingly few pastors gauge the value of a worship event by outcomes such as sensitivity to the Holy Spirit, facilitating a worshipful environment, or fostering God's presence. The typical pastor wants people to get something out of the components of the service that precede the sermon but is most concerned about the perceived value of the sermon itself.[6]

Expected outcomes among the laity. Most people attend worship events expecting to experience outcomes such as comfort, predictability, professionalism, and satisfying interpersonal relationships. Very few accept divine confrontation as a hallmark of worship. Yet, sometimes God uses a worship environment to grasp our attention and interact with us in ways that bring greater discomfort than security and joy. To most adults, such an experience is viewed as a negative, not a positive.[7]

> The problem is that American Christians do not have a heart that is thirsting for an experience with God, eager to express gratitude and praise to him, and open to his response to their efforts to convey humility, appreciation, acknowledgment of his love and character, and joy in knowing and serving him.

Put this in context, and the notion that America has a major problem in the area of worship is an inescapable conclusion. Perhaps the most striking feature of the research is the revelation that our problem is not an inability to craft services or experiences that are culturally relevant—we know how to do that, although many churches still resist doing so. The problem is that American Christians do not have a heart that is thirsting for an experience with God, eager to express gratitude and praise to him, and open to his response to their efforts to convey humility, appreciation, acknowledgment of his love and character, and joy in knowing and serving him.

Cultural Influences on Worship

If worship is so central to the Christian experience, then how is it possible for churched people to have strayed so far from the mark? In large part it is because the cultural context guides our worship expectations and practices, rather than the other way around. Given that most people attending church services are clueless as to the true meaning of worship, and because relatively few have actually experienced genuine worship during their lifetime, the common experiences and perspectives emanating from the culture shape even that which occurs within the most hallowed of church events, the worship service.

It's not difficult to reconstruct the avalanche of influences that dictate people's views about God, faith, and worship. Consider just a few societal trends and conditions and how they define people's worship endeavors.

• Ethnic diversification has brought about a splintering of worship approaches to satisfy the unique needs and perspectives of various ethnic groups.

• Differences in approaches to faith, understanding of worship, and personal styles of faith engagement based upon generational divisions, have resulted in distinctive styles of worship. In many cases, it is nearly impossible to get people from different age groups to meaningfully worship together.

• Functional illiteracy, which affects approximately half of our adult population, has left millions of individuals ignorant of the content of worship. Many are incapable of reading the Bible, liturgy, hymnals, and related resources. Millions cannot comprehend the content of the sermons preached at the services they attend.

• A majority of the people who attend churches contend that there is no such thing as absolute moral truth. This has produced a nation of churchgoers who accept only portions of the teaching to which they are exposed, and literally millions who question the truth of the Bible on which their faith is based. Such a perspective also minimizes the significance of evangelistic appeals made during worship services.

• Shifting values have altered the feel, the content, and the conduct of many services in order to remain appealing, relevant, and helpful. Among the widely embraced values that have influenced worship practices are people's demand for convenience, for decision-making participation, for time efficiency, for professionalism in presentation, for relational intimacy, and for personalization of experiences.

• The rejection of the uniqueness of Christian theology and perspective—as manifested in beliefs that all major faiths teach the same lessons, that there is not a "right" faith, that people of all faiths have the same post-life outcome, that it doesn't matter what faith you belong to, and that people of all different faiths pray to the same God regardless of the name they attach to that deity—has reshaped worship.

• The rise of megachurches has altered the worship styles of small and medium-sized churches, in their effort to compete or to be "relevant." This has resulted in shifts toward "blended" worship, shorter services, therapeutic preaching, and the de-emphasis of tithing.[8]

Naturally when lifestyle trends and culturally influenced expectations dictate the nature of a corporate worship endeavor, more than just the methodology changes: Worship content and experience are transformed as well.

Stirrings in Worship

The factors described above help to explain why worship has undergone such dramatic changes in the past several decades. In fact, if we were to track the progression of corporate worship experiences over the past half-century we would identify a vast number of pivotal shifts in churchwide worship practices. Major changes include:

Styles of music. Tens of thousands of churches have transitioned from utilizing hymns, organs, and robed choirs led by a music leader to praise choruses, keyboards, bands, and a small vocal team directed by a worship leader. The music is often completed in a prolonged block of time, rather than separated by announcements, testimonies, introductions, and other items on the agenda.

Construct of the service. There is a much greater concern about continuity and flow in services than has traditionally been true. With people exposed to professional entertainment on a regular basis through television, movies, and other means, the competition for people's allegiance and attention has raised the bar in terms of the quality of "performance," whether the component in question is the sermon, the music, or other presentational and interactive aspects.

Preaching style. Preachers are being pushed in two dimensions. First, people are less willing to accept sermons that do not provide practical applications for their life. Sermons focusing on mere exegesis of Scripture, without concurrent strategies for doing something with that knowledge, have become repulsive to millions of churchgoers. Second, sermons must reflect the communication styles that are appreciated by the audience segment that is being addressed. For instance, while Gen Xers prefer stories, interactive communication, and a dialogical approach; Baby Boomers, in contrast, respond best to empirical information, logical arguments, and references to experience. Builders more readily accept sermons that are pedantic and purely exegetical.

Dress styles. Church used to be a place where people attended in their finest clothing, sometimes becoming more of a fashion show than a worship experience. These days church has become much more casual; the focus is placed more upon how we interact with

God than how we dress up for him.

These days the focus is placed more upon how we interact with God than how we dress up for him.

Participation. These days, people want to participate. Growing numbers of people desire to be emotionally and intellectually involved in the process of worship. Enabling people to converse with each other during the service, incorporating times for healing or commitment, providing public prayer times and other forms of personal expression are more common now than in the past.

Use of technology. Having moved away from hymnals to more contemporary music, churches provide the words to songs through the use of overhead projectors or big-screen projection systems that utilize computers. Rather than natural sound, churches often spend hundreds of thousands of dollars on elaborate sound systems. Stationary microphones attached to a pulpit have been replaced by lapel mikes or, in some cases, headsets. Larger churches frequently utilize theater-style lighting. Announcements are sometimes made through videotaped information and music. By displaying children's sign-in numbers on an electronic board mounted on a wall in the sanctuary, church staff can notify parents of young children who are struggling in their Sunday school classes; parents can then return to their children during the service and tend to their needs. Security personnel have been replaced by laser-based alarm systems.

Scheduling. While most churches still offer their services on Sunday morning, the times have become a bit more flexible. Increasing numbers of churches offer services on other days, too. Saturday afternoon and evening services have become commonplace, although on each of the other days of the week there are churches throughout the nation that provide worship events.

Facility design. Once upon a time you could travel from city to city, attend worship services at different churches, and feel comforted by the familiarity of the sanctuary design. These days, facilities are functional more than aesthetic, resulting in a plethora of interior designs characterizing churches. Many growing churches have moved to a multipurpose sanctuary, using stackable chairs that can be easily removed or reconfigured depending on the next event for which the auditorium will be used. A popular approach for larger churches is to replicate a theater environment using hinged, cushioned chairs and carpeted aisles facing the bare stage area. Stained-glass windows are passé in most places; tinted glass, perhaps, with electronically controlled window coverings is the choice for more modern facilities.

Those who last attended a church service in the 1950s or even 1960s would be shocked by what a present-day worship service looks like, sounds like, and feels like in thousands of churches across the land. In fact, our research shows that many of those people are not only caught off guard by the worship facility when they do visit after an extended absence, but are pleasantly surprised by the updating that has occurred in the worship environment.

Addressing the Problems

While all these changes are interesting and may serve valid purposes, the underlying issue remains unchanged: Far more people attend worship services than actually worship God at those services. How can churches solve this important dilemma?

By studying the churches that have a superior track record at facilitating genuine worship, we have discovered several practices that seem significant in explaining their success. The churches that have established highly effective approaches to worship have not only prioritized worship, but have also created ways of enabling people to engage in real worship. In a few cases these churches hit on an approach that worked from day one; in more instances, the procedures they embraced were the result of an arduous and sometimes painful trial-and-error process. You have to give these churches credit for assigning great importance to worship, for recognizing that they had a serious worship problem, for their willingness to adopt innovative or uncomfortable changes in worship practices, and for their diligence in solving their problems. [9]

The churches that have established highly effective approaches to worship have not only prioritized worship, but have also created ways of enabling people to engage in real worship.

We found that a common obstacle to facilitating real worship is that the church's leaders do not understand what worship is—and isn't. Despite seminary education and denominational guidance, a shockingly high number of church leaders have no real understanding or philosophy of worship; they merely continue the routines that they have experienced for years and years without any questions or concerns about viability and impact. How can we shatter such neglectful conformity toward instituting minds and hearts that yearn for God, that connect with God, and that enjoy the presence of God through worship activities?

Certainly, before a congregation is likely to enter into true worship, the church's leaders must be very clear as to what worship means (concept) and how to achieve a worshipful state (practice). If the intent is to usher people into God's presence, this often demands that the leaders of the ministry reconceptualize the meaning and purpose of worship; re-engineer how worship events are designed and conducted; and implement a simple, but reliable method of evaluating what has transpired at the worship event.

These fundamental needs have raised some controversial and

difficult questions within the church. Among the questions still ve-hemently debated among Christian leaders—and deserving of such discussion and reflection—are the following:

• What is the meaning of worship?

• What is the role of the local church in bringing a worshipper into God's presence?

• What role does the Holy Spirit play in a worship service?

• Is creating a service that is "relevant" to the prevailing culture thereby "selling out" to that culture?

• What role, if any, should the laity play in creating the worship experience?

• Does real worship emphasize sensitivity and flexibility or struc-ture and order in its design—or both?

• Is it even possible to measure the effectiveness of worship? If it is, what criteria are reasonable, and how is such information to be collected?

• Do people who attend a worship service worship by virtue of their presence at the event? If not, how can they be taught the true meaning and experience of biblical worship?

• What are the distinct responsibilities of the worshippers and of the church?

• Can people who have not fully devoted themselves to Jesus Christ actually worship a God whom they do not know in a personal, significant way?

• Do seeker events undermine the necessity for and people's per-sonal investment in a truly worshipful experience?

• What are people's expectations regarding worship? What are the expectations of clergy and other church leaders?

• What distinction, if any, must be understood between corporate worship and personal worship?

• What is the role of music in worship? Does the style really make a difference? Is "blended worship" a viable option if true worship, rather than pandering to the audience, is the objective?

• Can a lecture (the typical sermon) facilitate true worship? If so, how?

• Does confession of our sins have a role in worship?

• How does the worship environment impact people's ability to relate to God?

• How does one's fundamental theological precepts influence the practice of worship?

• What does it take to develop a holistic, internally consistent philosophy of worship—if such an endeavor is even desirable?

By conscientiously studying, praying, evaluating, experimenting, and growing in reference to these questions, thousands of churchgoers have discovered ways of contextualizing what they do in worship without compromising what they stand for as representatives and practitioners of the Christian faith. But reaching the place of efficacy in worship is not a simple matter. The lesson grasped by churches that consistently facilitate authentic corporate worship is that providing such an experience in the midst of a culture that is so complex, fluid, and antithetical to the worship of God, requires clarity of purpose, substantial effort, the courage to experiment and grow, and diligence.

Helping the People

Given the struggle of most churchgoers to have a positive worship experience, we found that the churches most effective in worship take certain steps toward helping their people worship. First, they realize that worship is an unnatural act in a postmodern culture; indeed, it's virtually countercultural. Teaching individuals how to worship by helping them achieve a sense of God's holiness, understand the meaning of worship, and commit to worshipping God is often necessary if more than just a scattered handful of attendees are to be engaged in real worship. Perhaps your church doesn't struggle with the factors confronted by the most worshipful churches in America, but these are valuable considerations to take into account.

Can people worship a God they don't know? Most of the churches we worked with concluded that it wasn't likely. Consequently, one of the emphases of those successful churches was to do everything possible to enable each attendee to have a truly vibrant, grace-based relationship with Jesus Christ. Having such a relationship doesn't automatically enable a person to worship God on a regular basis, but it certainly provides a strong foundation for genuine worship.

But once individuals are open to worship, they still must be taught the reasons for worship, the content of worship, and the internal spiritual dynamics of worship. This entails more than showing up at the right time on Sunday morning. Unless people deeply understand the purposes of worship, they are likely to lose interest in the act and to engage in sloppy, halfhearted interaction with God. Until they comprehend all that worship encompasses, they are likely to sit back in their comfortable chairs and watch a religious performance unfold before them. And if they haven't come with hearts that are seeking to connect with the heart of their Creator and to experience

Unless people deeply understand the purposes of worship, they are likely to lose interest in the act and to engage in sloppy, halfhearted interaction with God.

God in an intimate and powerful way, then they're not likely to persevere in the act of worshipping.

Diversity in Worship

One of the most unfortunate questions asked by many church leaders is, What is the best method of worshipping? It's unfortunate because it betrays their misunderstanding of worship. Too many pastors and congregational leaders view worship as a series of definable, unchanging, one-dimensional steps that may be copied from churches that regularly meet God and integrated into the existing framework of ministry activities at their churches.

Worship is an extension of the organizing purpose of a church as determined by the mission, vision, and values that define the church and form the cornerstone of its call to existence. Worship philosophy, format, and evaluation are natural extensions of those central principles. The means of communicating a valid understanding of worship stems from those principles. The ways in which worship is evaluated are inextricably related to the church's mission, vision, and values—and, consequently, may be completely unique to that ministry.[10]

This means that some churches appropriately utilize seeker services as a means of developing future followers of Christ, who will then worship with fervor (in a different worship setting). For other churches a tradition-saturated, liturgical format is entirely consistent with the vision and heartbeat of their ministries. For others, a variety of alternative worship ventures are reasonable, including entertainment-oriented worship; silent, reflective, deliberately paced worship; low-process, hyper-relational forms; cyber-worship; house church and cell group worship experiences; dialogical worship; Pentecostal worship incorporating the charismatic gifts; and so forth. None of these approaches is superior or more theologically valid than another; what matters is their consistency with the Bible, their ability to connect people with God, and the pleasure that those practices bring to God.

It is also becoming increasingly common for a church to have multiple worship services—and for each service to utilize a different approach. Does that reflect manipulation? pandering? spiritual compromise? In most cases, this is a simple recognition that even with a given mission, vision, and set of core values, divergent means of facilitating worship is possible—and healthy. Rather than prevent people from connecting with God because a particular style or approach to worship doesn't meet everyone's needs, the multiple-services, distinct-styles strategy demonstrates the significance those churches attach to people achieving an intimate connection with God. The use of different approaches to worship in different services is not so much selling out as it is evidence of the prioritization and appropriate contextualization of worship.

And this chapter would be incomplete without reference to the fact that the most worshipful churches in our land also promote the notion of constant personal worship—that is, worship as a lifestyle offered to God apart from a corporate event. If our lives are to be a blessing to God and to reflect how dearly we honor and praise him, then we must view and live our every thought, word, and deed through the lens of worship. As you can imagine, churches that have enabled their people to own the principle of lifestyle worship have a much easier time of facilitating congregation-wide worship when the corporate worship event occurs.[11]

Do people need to interact with God in worship? Indisputably, yes! Do Americans want to worship God? Fortunately, the answer remains affirmative, although most Americans have little understanding of what they're seeking in the practice and experience of worship. The bottom line is that in a spiritually starved nation like ours, people want to have a real relationship with the God who created them. They want to express their love to the One who loves them. They're willing to design their weekly schedule to fit a corporate worship experience that enables them to experience and respond to the powerful, life-transforming presence of God. Let's pray that while the window of opportunity remains open we may exploit the inner yearning that millions possess to be intimately connected with their Father in heaven through genuine, authentic, consistent, purposeful, loving, and pleasing expressions of worship.

NOTES

1. OmniPoll 99-1, a nationwide survey among a random sample of 1005 adults, conducted January 1999 by the Barna Research Group, Ltd. of Ventura, CA. For these and similar survey results, consult the Barna Research Web site: www.barna.org.

2. This is based upon a nationwide survey among a random sample of 1003 adults, conducted in August 1997 by the Barna Research Group, Ltd.

3. Random sample of 1003 adults, August 1997, Barna Research Group, Ltd.

4. Random sample of 1003 adults, August 1997, Barna Research Group, Ltd.

5. Random sample of 1003 adults, August 1997, Barna Research Group, Ltd.

6. There are a variety of studies we have conducted to arrive at this conclusion. The most recent of these was PastorPoll 1997, a nationwide survey of a random sample of 610 Protestant senior pastors.

7. These challenges are discussed in greater detail in the audiotaped presentation "Facilitating Genuine Worship," by George Barna, Barna Research Group, 1998. It is available from the Barna Research Group, 5528 Everglades St., Ventura, CA 93003; 805-658-8885; or via the Web site: www.barna.org.

8. For a more extensive discussion of these trends, see *The Second Coming of the Church,* by George Barna, Word Books, Nashville, TN, 1998.

9. This research and the solutions applied by these churches is described in chapter 5 of *The Habits of Highly Effective Churches,* George Barna, Issachar Resources, Ventura, CA, 1998. The book is available from the Barna Research Group.

10. This holistic approach to ministry—using the mission, vision, and values as the cornerstone from which all ministry philosophy, practices, and evaluations are developed—is one of the hallmarks of the most effective ministry leaders and of the most

effective ministries in America. Our research among those types of leaders and ministries and how others may adopt a similar approach to developing an internally consistent, vision-based ministry, is contained in *Turning Vision Into Action,* George Barna, Regal Books, Ventura, CA, 1996.

11. The Bible speaks to the issue of living a life of worship to God. Among the more direct references are Romans 12:1; Psalm 42:1-2; Jeremiah 9:23-24; Colossians 3:1-2; Matthew 22:37-40; 1 Corinthians 10:31. A helpful book in this regard is *Lifestyle Worship,* John Garmo, Thomas Nelson Publishers, Nashville, TN, 1993.

Chapter 2

Convergence Worship:

A Blending of Traditions

by ROBERT WEBBER

I n 1990 when Keith Gaddis became the music minister of Maryland Community Church in Terre Haute, Indiana, he inherited a scenario found in many churches: two services—one traditional, the other contemporary.[1]

Keith immediately began to talk about converging the traditional and the contemporary, and on occasion he planned and led a blended style so people could see what it looked like. Because of the positive response, he continued to introduce blended worship until the convergence style of worship was fully established.

In a recent phone conversation with Keith, I said, "You know as I do that some teachers in the church are saying to stay away from convergence worship, that there's something in it to offend everyone."

Keith laughed. "I don't think so," he said. "Not for me."

"What proof do you have?" I asked.

"Well, first of all, let's look at the numerical statistics. I don't want to overemphasize numbers because the real impact on our church has been the deepening of our spirituality. But everyone seems interested in numerical growth, so I'll start there."

"OK," I said. "What happened?"

"When I came in 1990 we had an average attendance of 326 people at either the traditional or contemporary service. In 1990 I began to teach on blended worship and experimented with it to give people an idea of what it looked like. We then went full throttle with blended worship and the growth curve shot up dramatically."

"How dramatically?"

"From 1990 to 1998 we went from 326 people to 1,431 people. This is more than a four-time growth in eight years."

Because I wasn't satisfied with only growth statistics, I asked Keith, "What are some of the things you do in worship that make an impact on people?" His comments ranged from music to pageantry to the liturgical calendar to symbolism.

First, *music* plays an important role in renewal worship.

"I truly respect and love our new music" said Keith, "but we can't ignore the place of the great hymns and gospel songs in the history of the church."

Those who take a marketing approach to the church and its worship caution against mixing traditional and contemporary styles of music. But Keith reports a different experience. According to him, "Historical music is very appealing to the churched and unchurched if it's done with the same musical energy that we give to contemporary music." The key to Gaddis' statement is *the same musical energy*. Listless singing reflects a less than enthusiastic congregation, whereas enthusiastic singing speaks of an enthusiastic and committed congregation of committed Christians.

Second, Keith has found that *pageantry* captures the imagination of the people. He understands the shift that has taken place in communication from the exclusive emphasis on the verbal to a recovery of the visual. "I want to enhance the visual experience of worship," he says. "We use bright and beautiful banners in procession. On any given Sunday you'll see striking banners bearing phrases such as 'Bright Morning Star,' 'Bread of Life,' 'Wonderful Counselor,' 'King of Kings,' and 'I Am the Resurrection and the Life.'" These banners "communicate a sense of transcendence, the otherness of the God who is among us."

Next, Maryland Community Church makes the *celebrations* of the Christian year special. As Keith says, "These are the events that mark out and celebrate the great saving events of God in history. Because these liturgies are marked by great music and visual praise, the people are led to a deeper acknowledgment and understanding of the meaning of salvation."

Finally, Keith points to the recovery of *symbolism* as a crucial element of worship renewal. Maryland Community Church uses symbolism in a powerful way to emphasize the church calendar year. For example, during Lent, Keith states, "We use a dark cloth draped over the cross to signify our sins. Then from Easter Sunday through Pentecost we proclaim together, 'He is risen! He is risen! He is risen!' And we change the dark cloth on the cross to white to signify Jesus' victory over our sins through his death and resurrection."

Maryland Community Church is one example of the many churches blending the great treasures of historic worship with contemporary worship. In this chapter, our study of convergence worship is divided into three parts: In part 1, I deal with the theology of blended worship. My concern is to make sure that our theology of worship is rooted in Scripture and honors the traditions of worship given to us by the Holy Spirit. In part 2, I deal with the revolution taking place in culture. Worship has always been related to culture and that issue can't be ignored in our current worship renewal. However, worship isn't something we reinvent every time culture changes. Instead, as I will show, the content remains the same, while it's the style that changes from culture to culture. Finally, in part 3, I present three models of convergence worship: a liturgical model, a traditional Protestant model, and a contemporary model.

Let's begin where we ought to begin—with an understanding of what worship is all about.

Part 1: The Theology of Worship

There is no finer definition of worship than the *Te Deum* (Latin for "You are God"). The *Te Deum* is a prayer that dates from the fourth century and represents a high point in the development of a theology of worship (for the full text of the prayer, see "Te Deum" on page 53).[2]

Although the origin of the prayer can't be traced, the content of the prayer and its understanding of worship are rooted in Scripture and in the development of early Christian thought. The themes of God's transcendence, God's glory in creation, and God's actions throughout salvation history dominate the *Te Deum* and give us insight into the content of worship in the early church. *Te Deum* is a prayer, and this fact calls attention to the forgotten reality that worship is primarily prayer. Worship is a prayer of relationship in which the whole creation lauds and magnifies God, the Creator and Redeemer of the world. Unfortunately, many congregations don't envision worship as a prayer; instead, worship is seen primarily as outreach or edification. Prayer worship bids us to acknowledge as Soren Kierkegaard once noted, "If there is an audience in worship, it is God." *Te Deum* calls us to rid ourselves of the language of stage, audience, and performance. Worship is a dramatic expression of God's glory and a representation of God's saving deeds in history for which we, the community of God's people on earth, offer grateful praise and thanksgiving.

A second key to worship as expressed by *Te Deum* is that there's a place where worship is eternally happening. That place is in the heavens. When we worship we join the heavenly throng, the angels and archangels, the cherubim and the seraphim, and the whole company of saints including the prophets, the apostles, and the martyrs. Jesus alludes to this eternal place of worship in his conversation with the Samaritan woman: "A time is coming when you will worship the Father neither on this mountain nor in Jerusalem…when the true worshipers will worship the Father in spirit and truth" (John 4:21, 23). Repudiating the common Jewish places of worship, Jesus locates the place of worship in the Spirit. The "spirit" is understood biblically to be the eternal place of worship around the throne, where continual worship is offered to God. When we worship, we ascend into the heavens and join heavenly worship.

In the New Testament, John wrote of a similar experience: "On the Lord's Day I was in the Spirit [the heavenly place]" (Revelation 1:10). "At once I was in the Spirit, and there before me was a throne in heaven with someone sitting on it" (Revelation 4:2). The whole book of Revelation is primarily about worship and the praise that belongs to God because of God's ultimate overthrow of the powers of evil. The liturgies of the early church follow this pattern of entering into heavenly worship, particularly at the Eucharist when the congregation joins the heavenly throng to sing *The Sanctus* and to recall God's mighty deeds of salvation.

Third, *Te Deum* teaches us that the worship of God is not the worship of an essence, who simply sits in the heavens. It's the worship of a God who not only creates but also becomes personally involved in creation. Worshipping God as the creator is an essential part of worship; the psalms are full of such creator praise (see Psalms 8; 19; 65; 104; 148). Following in the tradition of the psalms, the liturgy of the synagogue and early Christian worship was also full of creator praise. Worship also celebrated God's actions in history, whereby the created order was rescued after the Fall. God will also come in Jesus Christ to destroy all the powers of evil and to establish a new heaven and a new earth.

In sum, through worship we ascend into the heavens and join the heavenly hosts to proclaim the glory of God. We acclaim God as creator, we remember God's mighty deeds of salvation, and we anticipate God's final victory over evil and the establishment of God's eternal kingdom. Through the words and actions of worship, the world which is dislocated is relocated through God's redeeming acts. The order of creation, from creator to created, is established in its intended form. This is the essence of worship as understood by the early church and, if recovered today, has the power to revolutionize our worship and change the modern church.

The second aspect of a theology of worship is the structure of public worship. At first glance it would appear that structure or the order of worship is not related to a theology of worship. We tend to think of the structure of worship as a description, not a prescription.

The primary principle for the ordering of public worship is to remember that worship on the human side is a rehearsal of our relationship to God.

For example, in many churches worship is organized as a program. It consists of a series of acts of worship that appear in a willy-nilly way. The worship planner says, Let's see…we need a hymn, a prayer, a solo. And often, without any thought to the inner coherence of worship, the planner develops a program of worship events. This approach to worship eventually lends itself to "entertainment," where worship is directed to the congregation and not to God.

The primary principle for the ordering of public worship is to remember that worship on the human side is a rehearsal of our relationship to God. This idea shows up in the first act of public worship recorded in the Bible. Moses is called by God to (1) assemble the people at the mountain, (2) hear the word of the Lord, (3) enter into an agreement with God based on sacrifice and a meal, and (4) go forth into the world to live out of this relationship (Exodus 24:1-8). This fourfold pattern of relationship is found in every covenant of Scripture, including the covenant established by Jesus at the Last Supper in Matthew 26:17-30 (preparation, spoken word, meal, going out). Furthermore, liturgical scholarship points to Luke 24 as the most insightful New Testament passage on the content and order of worship. They were "going to a village," and as they walked on the road "he explained to them what was said in all the Scriptures concerning himself," then he was recognized by them when he broke the bread. They cried, "We knew him in the breaking of the bread" when they arrived at Jerusalem. This is why the earliest liturgies of the church focused on Word and Table: Luke tells us "they devoted themselves to the apostles' teaching and to the fellowship, to the breaking of the bread and to prayer" (Acts 2:42).

Content and structure are brought together when we plan worship as a rehearsal of our relationship to God. It contains all the God-directed elements of Christian truth and all the dimensions of human response. We enter into a divine-human encounter as we assemble in God's presence, hear God's Word, respond with bread and wine in thanksgiving, and go forth into the world to love and serve the Lord (see "A Model for Worship" on page 54).

This model, which draws from early Christian worship, is a good model for blending the historic substance of worship with the evangelical spirit. Its "form" incorporates the substance of historic Christianity, yet provides for the freedom and spontaneity characteristic of contemporary Christianity. It avoids on the one hand the deadness of mere repetition and on the other hand a zealous enthusiasm which neglects form and content.

Part 2: Our Changing World

I've argued above that the content and order of worship don't change because they're characterized by a "transcultural value." Because the content and structure of worship are firmly rooted in Scripture and in the early church tradition, they endure in every paradigm of history, in every culture, in all geographical locations, and at all times. What changes is style. And style is rooted in culture. A glimpse of worship and its relationship to culture since 1950 will help us understand this principle better.

World War II marked a turning point in Western history. The change was so dramatic and far-reaching that most people agree with C.S. Lewis that we now live in "the post-Christian era." Today's world is strikingly similar to the time when the Christian faith emerged in the Roman Empire. People then and now turn to the gods of astrology and to the extreme even embrace evil powers in order to experience spirituality. The current longing for spiritual experience says that we Christians must seize the moment. We can do so through a worship that restores the biblical and historical supernaturalism—a worship that's inviting and participatory, bringing meaning and healing to life.

Keith Gaddis discovered this kind of worship. For him and Maryland Community Church, worship stands at the center of the church's life and mission. It's the summit toward which the church moves and the source from which all of its ministries flow. It's the most important action the church is about. Worship informs the church's teaching, gives shape to its evangelistic mission to the world, and compels the church toward social action. Worship is the context in which the true fellowship of Christ's body is realized and where those who participate can find real healing.

> *The single most important thing the church can do is worship.*

The single most important thing the church can do is worship. A vibrant worship life will glorify God, edify the faithful, and engage the seeker. Convergence worship can accomplish these goals. But first, before looking at this kind of worship, we need to understand why so many people find the current worship of some churches spiritually dead and unsatisfying.

Why Does Worship Seem So Dead?

The problems we experience in worship are directly related to our enlightenment worldview and its anti-supernatural and rationalistic perspective on life.

For example, the Western world lives out a secular story that goes like this: The world came into existence by chance. It's a huge machine capable of being understood through rational inquiry and investigation. Human beings must create the world's future. The meaning of life must emerge out of the choices we humans make.

It was the voices of the Enlightenment that proclaimed this world could be understood by the human mind. Darwin introduced the notion of evolution, an idea soon applied to the chance origin of the world and of the human species. Then Freud argued that religion was the invention of the human imagination, born out of the weakness of humans who needed a supernatural crutch to survive life. Finally, Karl Marx, the third influential figure of the nineteenth century, said human beings must take history into their own hands. They must shape their own future by eliminating the competition between the rich and the poor and create a new communal society where all people will live in harmony under a loving government.

During the last half of the twentieth century various worship responses may be interpreted in light of secularism. The liberals pandered to the secularists and shed worship of its supernatural nature. The traditional conservatives turned worship into a defense of the supernatural, but lost the sense of mystery. Contemporary worship broke with tradition to create an entertainment worship based on pop culture that would hopefully attract the seeker.

However, since the 1990s, our culture has been undergoing another very significant change. Darwin, Freud, and Marx are no longer the heroes of society. Instead, we're witnessing a shift into a new age of spirituality and mysticism. Because the church hasn't changed significantly, "going to church" is irrelevant for many. The issues that became prominent in the 1990s will become central in the twenty-first century. They're different than the issues of the sixties, seventies and eighties. In a word, we have moved into the postmodern, post-Christian era. Consequently, an understanding of the revolutions that have brought us where we are is indispensable to an understanding of the kinds of changes taking place in the style of our worship.

The first challenge comes from the twentieth-century revolution in science. The mechanistic worldview of the Enlightenment and the high estimate of human reason to ultimately understand the way the world works began to break down with the smashing of the atom. While it was once thought "the world stands still," now we know that nothing stands still; everything is in perpetual motion. This new science with its movement away from rational comprehension opened the door to mystery once again. The world now appears to be complex and mysterious.

Next, the shift from a mechanistic worldview to an open and dynamic world in perpetual motion forces us to think differently about our world. The world is now seen as a dynamic and interactive world. We're all interconnected and can no longer claim to be detached observers of a life going on outside ourselves. We're participants in a community.

Third, the revolution in communications has made a powerful impact on society. In the modern world communication occurred primarily through conceptual knowledge. Words that dominated the ways of knowing were "reading," "writing," "intelligence," "analysis," "clarity," "explanation," "logic," and "linear sequence." The new postmodern shape of communication has shifted to a more symbolic form. It is knowledge gained through personal participation in a community. The new catch phrases include "the primacy of experience," "knowledge through immersed participation," the "impact of the visual" (such as atmosphere, environment, and space), the rediscovery of "imagination" and "intuition," and a sensitivity to "spiritual realities."

These three revolutions have literally changed the landscape of the world. And the shifts they've introduced have a direct bearing on worship. In science we've shifted from the extreme of rationalism to an affirmation of mystery. In philosophy the shift is from individualism to community. In communications our society has shifted from a focus on the verbal to a more symbolic form of communication.

The reason why so many people find worship boring is simply this: In our life in the world, we're aware of mystery,

The reason why so many people find worship boring is simply this: In our life in the world, we're aware of mystery, community, and symbol. But the majority of churches are still operating out of the old style of rationalism, individualism, and verbal communication.

community, and symbol. But the majority of churches are still operating out of the old style of rationalism, individualism, and verbal communication. We've attempted to make the mystery of God understandable. We've turned worship into something we "watch" instead of "do." And our worship is dominated by words, words, words. Our worship style is that of the old world view, not that of the postmodern world.

However, since the late 1960s, attempts have been made to change the style of worship in keeping with the changing patterns of culture. A brief survey of these changing styles will help us understand where style is headed in culture and in the church.

The Changing Culture

Sociologists make helpful distinctions between the Boosters (born between 1927-1946), the Boomers (born between 1946-1961), the Busters (born between 1961-1981), and the Millennials (born since 1981). Studies show that each of these groups have been shaped by different cultural factors.

The Boosters are for the most part traditionalists. There were teenagers during the Eisenhower years. Society was stable, predictable and change came slowly and imperceptibly. Worship was always the same. In most conservative circles, worship consisted of singing hymns, preaching a sermon and giving an invitation. It was also nonconfrontive, seldom speaking to social and political issues. The concentration was on personal sin and need of a Savior.

Then came the social upheaval of the 1960s. President Kennedy wanted to "get this country moving again." And move it did: Protests over the Vietnam War. the civil rights movement, and sexual freedom led to "do your own thing." This attitude is still evident among the

1960s youth, who are now moving into middle age. They wanted freedom. During this same time we witnessed the conversion of the hippie and the emergence of the "Jesus movement." These new Christians embraced the content of the Christian faith, but embedded it within an antiestablishment style. Worship shifted to the casual, to the familiar and to the musical instrumentation of pop society. Organs were out. Guitars were in. Formality was out. Informality was in. Many of these Boomers followed the cultural values of the seventies and the eighties. They worked to translate everything into bigness—big corporations, big houses, big cars and big churches. Out of this philosophy they birthed the megachurch movement to serve every aspect of society and to meet all felt needs.

However, something significant happened in the late 1990s. As the Busters and Millennials found their voice, the children of the Boomers looked at their parents' generation and decided, as one teenager said to me, "That's not us. We don't want to be like our parents' generation." Greg Warner, the editor of Faith Works, a new magazine reflecting the attitudes of the Millennials, says, "Their skepticism and distrust of success and bigness will bring a needed corrective to the Boomers preoccupation with 'supersizing' everything." But Warner speaks also of an "overriding concern" for the Millennial generation and "its disdain for all things Boomer."[3]

Warner offers other valuable insights we must take into account as our culture is once again changing before our very eyes. "Millennials," he writes, "will be the first generation raised in a purely postmodern culture." The new epistemology of postmodernism "leaves an open door to mystery." Millennials are "willing to live with paradoxes." Their "eclectic bent allows them to reach back to historical expressions of the faith and mix those freely with their own cultural expressions." Warner also sees other hopeful signs among the Millennials. In their emphasis on "relationship and relational evangelism, love is demonstrated, not just proclaimed" and their emphasis on "community is genuine." And finally, "Their visual style of learning and expression will help return art to worship."

This brief cultural survey seems to suggest that the current generation of young people will not remain in step with the Boomer style. They want content, tradition and stability; they're oriented toward community; they want to participate, be involved. And, having grown up in an audiovisual society, they're accustomed to symbolic and nonvisual forms of communication. In the worship style of these young people, we can clearly see the impact of the scientific revolution (from reason to mystery), the philosophical revolution (from individualism to community), and the communications revolution (from verbal discourse to symbolic forms of communication).

Now we must ask: What kind of worship reflects this generation? In terms of content we want to worship God, not our feelings about God or our experiences of God. In terms of structure, we want our relationship to God to be an ordered experience of coming into God's presence, hearing God speak, celebrating at the Table, and being sent forth into the world to love and serve the Lord. And the style of this worship will more than likely follow the culture of the Millennials—an eclectic mixture of the old and the new, a return to transcendence and the sense of mystery, the formation of community, and an increased emphasis on the arts.

> "The worship of the twenty-first century isn't the traditional worship of the Booster, nor the contemporary worship of the Boomer and early Buster, but a convergence of worship traditions molded by the latter Busters and Millennials, who are soon to become the leaders of our churches."

Therefore, the worship of the twenty-first century isn't the traditional worship of the Booster, nor the contemporary worship of the Boomer and early Buster, but a convergence of worship traditions molded by the latter Busters and Millennials, who are soon to become the leaders of our churches.

Part 3: Sample Churches With Convergence Worship

I have asked the leaders of three churches to present their forms of convergence worship. Therefore, we turn to examples of liturgical/convergence, traditional/convergence, and contemporary/convergence worship.

Liturgical/Convergence

The liturgical/convergence worship model is experienced at Church of the Resurrection in Glen Ellyn, Illinois, and described here by the music minister, John Fawcett:[4]

Church of the Resurrection is an independent Anglican church, with an Episcopalian (ECUSA) background. Our services adhere consistently to the order laid out in The Book of Common Prayer. While remaining within that framework, however, there is considerable freedom to incorporate the riches of various church traditions. Our congregation of about four hundred is well-educated, devout, eager to worship, and open to a wide range of artistic styles. The members come from widely diverse backgrounds—from Roman Catholic to Mennonite, Presbyterian to Baptist, Pentecostal to Vineyard—but they are united in their common love for God and their commitment to several basic features of church life: (1) The centrality of the Word of God proclaimed and taught; (2) the centrality of worship and historically based liturgy, including the regular administration of the sacraments of Baptism and Eucharist; (3) the importance of outreach and evangelism, particularly as manifested in healing ministries to the broken; and (4) the centrality of the presence of the Holy Spirit as embodied in the Church gathered.

To a visitor, one of the most immediately noticeable evidences of blended worship is the music. Since our church meets in a rented space, we have to print our weekly bulletins. This allows me, as the pastoral musician, to draw upon many traditions as I select the music to be sung congregationally. Whereas churches that use only one hymnal generally remain tied to the repertoire within that collection, I am free to reprint any hymn that is in the public domain and to obtain permission to do so for the ones that are not. Because we believe in the historical continuity of the church's worship, our church is committed to singing hymns and carols from many sources: Gregorian chants, German Lutheran chorales, Anglican hymns, nineteenth-century American carols, and Roman Catholic contemporary songs (such as by John Michael Talbot), along with liturgical music written by members of our own congregation. At a recent Sunday morning service, we opened with an Anglican hymn, followed by two songs from the charismatic tradition published by Maranatha! Music, then a Gregorian chant a cappella. The offertory was an English translation of a sacred piece by Brahms for soprano, piano, and violin. During Communion, we sang a mix of hymns and contemporary songs, ending with a blues arrangement of a spiritual. Admittedly, this diversity could become dangerously centrifugal in its effect, but the common thread that unites our worship and preserves its unity is that it's directed God-ward. Each musical selection must be oriented to lifting our whole selves towards the One whom we are adoring. In his presence each variegated offering becomes, as it were, more truly itself, with its uniqueness amplified, but sharing with all of the other elements of the service in being an offering to God—not a "performance."

In preparing a worship service, I begin with an intimate knowledge of the liturgical structure of the service, including the boundaries of time that I must work within. I know where the service can "stretch" and where it must move along. I also give careful attention to which liturgical season we're celebrating. Each week the priest who is preaching will provide me with a sermon topic along with the lectionary readings for that Sunday in the church year. I read the Scripture passages prayerfully, jotting down those themes that appear most prominent to me and seeking to emphasize what I believe the Holy Spirit would lead us to focus on. Then I turn to selecting appropriate music, drawing on the repertoire with which the congregation is already familiar, while regularly introducing new music as well. I'll also consult the schedule of musicians for that Sunday, tailoring the selections to the particular instrumentation and mix of talent on the team that will be leading us in worship that week. I'm often amazed at how the Lord highlights something in our worship music that will perfectly complement the readings, the prayers, or the sermon topic. Despite my best efforts, these linkages would remain beyond human capacity to orchestrate.

In the flow of the liturgy itself, a visitor would also notice a blended style. Members of the congregation are free to clap and raise their hands, as in a charismatic church, but they also cross themselves at the reading of the Gospel, kneel for confession, and come forward to receive Communion from a common cup. Many of our sermons, though not all, are expository (part of our commitment to an evangelical heritage), yet we practice infant baptism—a sacramental view foreign to many evangelicals. At the conclusion of the service, anyone who wishes to receive prayer may approach a lay Communion minister for anointing with oil and the laying on of hands.

Visual elements and symbols also occupy a central place in the worship of the church. Acolytes process prior to the beginning of the liturgy to light the altar candles, symbolic of the light of Christ and his presence with us. Banners surround a central cross, which stand behind the Communion Table.

In addition, children follow a processional banner out of the adult service to participate in their own liturgy, which is adapted for their age group, but involves them not in entertainment but in encountering the presence of Jesus and entering into a loving relationship with him. Even the children begin to experience the importance of symbol as they put on "robes of righteousness" and belts with beads on them that represent the virtues.

Traditional/Convergence

Located in Olathe, Kansas, Christ Community is a start-up church in the Church of the Nazarene denomination. The report is written by the pastor, David Pendleton:[5]

Christ Community Church has its birth in the context of the Church of the Nazarene, a denomination rooted in the Holiness tradition, but whose "worship has been highly influenced in its historical development by the revivalistic approach to worship."[6] From its inception in 1908 until the mid-1960s, the pattern of worship varied little from congregation to congregation. For the most part this form of worship still remains rather intact today. Most worship services begin with an opening hymn, gospel song, pastoral prayer, announcements, offering, choir number, gospel song, "special music," sermon, and benediction (usually amounting to a recap of the sermon through the guise of closing prayer).

The experience tends to be emotionally driven and self-focused. In other words, we have gathered to be "fed" spiritually rather than to offer ourselves in worship to a holy God. There is little sense that the services are Christ-centered and little evidence of the historicity of the Christian church. In a service that is rather sermon-centered, we are "fortunate" to hear one passage of Holy Scripture. Holy Communion is viewed merely as a memorial and thus only celebrated once a quarter.

The Nazarene church began out of a desire for evangelism, a heart to serve the poor, and a place where holiness would be preached. Today there is a worship renewal taking place in the denomination—but driven mainly by current church growth principals and "successful" free-church models. Our church is a different model. Like other blended churches, we want to converge the historic with the contemporary.

Christ Community Church began in 1992 in a suburb of Kansas City with twenty-two people who had a passion to achieve substance and relevance in worship. We wanted to be a church whose worship is centered in Christ, biblical in its foundation, and embracing of the larger tradition of the Christian church. We knew that there was something more than what we had known and the answer to our internal "worship war" was not simply found in maintaining our tradition, becoming more contemporary, or even fully embracing a higher church liturgy as in our Wesleyan heritage. We do, after all, have ties to the Anglican tradition. John Wesley never ceased to be a priest in the Church of England. In fact, his heart was to revive the Church of England from within, not begin the Methodist movement. We believe, here at Christ Community, that we share a similar heart and that God's answer for our "internal struggle" could best be addressed in convergence worship—a "marriage" of worship movements drawn from the church's worship practices throughout history, centered in Christ, and empowered by the Holy Spirit to the praise of God. The answer was found in the diversity of our Christian worship practices; a bringing together of the liturgical/sacramental, evangelical, charismatic/pentecostal traditions into one worship experience. It's a convergence of worship practices without compromising the purpose of our gathering: to celebrate the life, death, and resurrection of Jesus and his victory over the powers of the enemy.

When the opportunity came my way to start a new church, I thought it would be the perfect setting to introduce the concept of convergence worship. The response has been quite favorable, and the worship services very meaningful. In fact, this approach to God in worship has become the driving central purpose of our church. By the means of blended worship, we are bringing people to Christ, developing their relationship with Christ, equipping them for works of service, and trusting the Holy Spirit to create a healthy church. God is being honored and lives are being changed. Our small committed core has grown from twenty-two people to over three hundred people who claim our church as their home. Thanks be to God!

Contemporary/Convergence

Valley Cathedral is a contemporary church in downtown Phoenix. This report comes from Dan Scott, the pastor:[7]

Valley Cathedral came into being because many of us found ourselves being rejected by the spiritual background in which we were born. God helped us to find one another. We had been Pentecostal, charismatic, Baptist, Catholic, Lutheran, Episcopal, and just plain heathen! For a long time we maintained our precious new unity by ignoring our divergent backgrounds. A few years ago we had matured to the place where we could begin to learn from one another.

The convergence began with me. I had come from a classical Pentecostal background. I sang black gospel. I sometimes "moaned" when I prayed. I wanted the freedom for that expression in our church. However, when I became a young adult, I discovered the evangelical churches. I admired the way they made the Word of God central to their services. They studied the Bible. I pleaded with our people that we too be evangelicals—people of the Word. A bit later I discovered the treasury of the liturgical tradition. Now, when I conduct a Communion service, I'm no longer happy about passing around some bread and wine in a flippant way. I try to give Communion the dignity that will call us to repentance and reverence. The Apostles' Creed also provided a good base for our common doctrinal expression. Soon all these things began to influence each other.

On each Sunday morning at 7:45, we have a very liturgical service in our old sanctuary. We have a presence light, a permanent altar that is located at the center of the chapel, and we worship in a sacramental, reverent way. Communion is served every Sunday. This part of our church also impacts the entire congregation on Communion Sunday, when we use a form of Rite Two in the Book of Common Prayer for the entire body. However, in the larger service, we use charismatic praise choruses liberally interspersed throughout the liturgy. We observe the church year. We treat ordination and marriage as sacramental, covenant-making ceremonies.

The church remains committed to vigorous Bible training and requires its leaders to go through a two-year study of the Scripture called The Bethel Series. In our two larger services on Sunday morning, and in the Spanish language service, our worship is more of an evangelical service with a charismatic flavor.

We continue to emphasize the charismatic aspects of our church life, especially during Pentecost and the following weeks and months. We are just beginning to use the Alpha course, developed by charismatic Anglicans in England, as our chief evangelistic tool. We attempt to teach our people a balanced but open heart to the sovereign divine unpredictability of the Holy Spirit.

Our commitment to convergence seemed to hurt us with every stream of Christian faith for a while. Now, however, it appears that the majority of Christian groups in our city respect our spiritual walk and wish us well. Our approach seems to be most effective for young adults, adventuresome people of all ages, and for those who desire an interracial Christian community.

After some years of difficulty and learning together, our people seem to be excited and motivated to learn, teach, and practice "the faith once delivered to the saints."

Conclusion

Throughout this chapter I've attempted to show that convergence worship is much more than the common opinion that it simply brings hymns and choruses together. It's first of all rooted in the content of historic worship and follows the structure of early Christian worship. In these two ways convergence worship reflects the liturgical scholarship of the twentieth century. However, in matters of style, convergence worship looks to the creative mixture of the old and new. It draws from the mystery of ancient worship, the centrality of the Word in reformation worship, the centrality of Christ and the emphasis on singing of the evangelicals and the concern for the intimacy and relationship of contemporary worship. I firmly believe this eclectic worship that emphasizes substance and relevance is the road to the future. It's biblical, embracing of historical development, and radically concerned for relevance.

NOTES

1. This material is taken from conversations and personal correspondence with Keith Gaddis.

2. This material has been adopted from Robert Webber, *Planning Blended Worship* (Nashville, TN: Abingdon, 1998), 13-34.

3. This and other quotes from Greg Warner are from personal correspondence.

4. Personal correspondence from John Fawcett.

5. Personal correspondence from David Pendleton.

6. *The Renewal of Sunday Worship*, 37.

7. Personal correspondence from Dan Scott.

TE DEUM

You are God and we praise you; you are the Lord and we acclaim you;

You are the eternal Father; all creation worships you.

To you all angels, all the powers of heaven,

Cherubim and seraphim sing in endless praise,

Holy holy holy Lord, God of power and might;

Heaven and earth are full of your glory.

The glorious company of apostles praise you;

The noble fellowship of prophets praise you;

The white-robed army of martyrs praise you.

Throughout the whole world the holy church acclaims you,

Father of majesty unbounded;

Your true and only Son worthy of all worship,

And the Holy Spirit advocate and guide,

You Christ are the King of glory,

The eternal Son of the Father.

When you became man to set us free

You did not abhor the virgin's womb.

You overcame the sting of death

And opened the kingdom of heaven to all believers.

You are seated at God's right hand in glory;

We believe that you will come and be our judge.

Come then Lord and help your people,

Bought with the price of your own blood;

And bring us with your saints

To glory everlasting.

A MODEL FOR WORSHIP

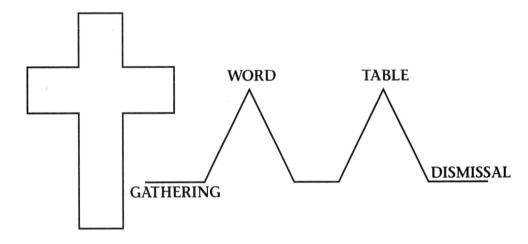

Convergence worship is primarily a proclamation and enactment of the Christ event. The fourfold pattern of worship gathers the people to proclaim God's Word, to offer praise and thanksgiving through enactment at the Table, and to go forth into the world to love and serve the Lord. This basic pattern of worship can be used by all churches everywhere as the style is adopted to the church's commitment to be formal, informal, or somewhere in between.

Chapter 3

Liturgical Worship:

Using Ritual to Inspire True Worship

by GARY M. BURGE

S ay "liturgy," and my students have a reflex akin to an invitation to take a quiz. But then say "mysticism," and they are drawn, fascinated, eager to see what I mean. At one moment, they recoil against perceived forms of fossilized religion. In the next, they yearn for experiences that transcend the commonplace evangelical forms of their upbringing. They want spontaneity, yet long for meaningful tradition in their lives. They enjoy going to church in blue jeans, but are intrigued by Christian meditation, spiritual disciplines honed in the medieval world, and candle-lit sanctuaries. Some play the latest "Chant" CD. Os Guiness, Saint Teresa of Avila, and Richard Foster might sit on their bookshelves. What exactly are these young seekers seeking?

Each June, Wheaton's Billy Graham Center hosts a weeklong healing ministry that focuses on mysticism and the inner life. It comes complete with banners, charismatic worship, inner healing, and meditative prayer and is hosted by the nationally known evangelist Leanne Payne.

Imagine the irony of it: Graham and Payne share as much in common as an ardent Southern Baptist and a charismatic Episcopalian.

One of my students named Karen is typical of these "seekers." She grew up in a large independent Bible church in the Midwest where she attended every youth camp and mission trip her family could find. Her role models came from the glossy pages of Campus Life magazine. When she came to Wheaton College she attended a large, influential, conservative evangelical church. But after a year her mind began to wander. "There was no imagination, no mystery, no beauty. It was all preaching and books and application," she told me. Today Karen is a senior and attends an Episcopal church nearby with a sizable group of her best friends.

Ask her if she likes liturgy and her eyes narrow: "Liturgy? Like in robes and candles and that sort of thing? Of course not." But I press, asking what she likes about the Episcopal church. "I truly worship there," she says. "It's the wonder, the beauty I love. I feel closer to God."

This week I finished reading my students' semester exams. One particularly insightful student, Amy Hassing, wrote about worship. "I think that much of modern society has lost a sense of divine, holy space," she writes. "This becomes obvious to me in our church architecture. The splendor and holiness of cathedrals which created the ultimate feeling of divine space has been replaced by gymnasiums and impermanent buildings. A sanctuary should be a place that is completely separate—that radiates the holiness of God. Plastic cups and folding chairs aren't enough. There has to be an environment that communicates God's holiness to my senses and to my spirit."

What's going on? What deficit, what experiential hunger in these students is not being met? What drives this irony—this rejection of "liturgy" while seeking the very elements in worship upon which all liturgy is built? What brings Payne to the Graham Center to minister to sold-out audiences? What leads countless students to attend a breakaway Episcopalian church (The Church of the Resurrection), where waving banners, The Book of Common Prayer, dance, guitars, ornate liturgical decor, and healing all work together?

One Wheaton faculty member who now worships at "The Church of the Rez" answered the question this way, "At last a place where I can find intelligent charismatic worship—with dignity."

This week I received a copy of *Rediscovering the Rich Heritage of Orthodoxy* (Light & Life). What amazed me is that it was written by an old friend with whom I studied at Fuller Seminary. His name is Charles Bell. "I have finally come home," he penned on the inside cover. And in the book he describes how this centuries-old, high liturgical church attracted a classical Pentecostal, former chaplain at Oral Roberts University who holds a Ph.D. in theology from Scotland and was ordained by the Vineyard Fellowship.

My pilgrimage is less dramatic but shares a common thread. I grew up in a Lutheran church, chiefly through the inspiration of my Swedish-Lutheran family. I still remember serving as a young acolyte, tending the mysteries of candle and altar and Communion Table. My Catholic high school friends wore "Saint Christopher" chains, but I had my own "I am a Lutheran" medallion (which I still keep along with some old "Nixon for President" buttons).

But when I entered the University of California, I met the "Jesus movement," a spiritual counterpart to the '60s counterculture. I followed them to Calvary Chapel in Costa Mesa, California, and witnessed something no Lutheran boy could imagine. It was a world of rock 'n' roll healing services in Hawaiian shirts, leather Bibles, and speaking in tongues by the thousands. I began to question my liturgical Lutheranism. When I entered Fuller Theological Seminary in 1974, the

In time I came to swim in the mainstream of evangelicalism. Soul-winning, hard-hitting sermons, and revival hymns became staples of my diet. But deep inside I knew that something was terribly wrong. Something was missing. My friends bravely proclaimed the certainty of evangelical theology, but somewhere the mystery of God was lost.

charismatic renewal was in full swing, and again, the diversity of the church and nonliturgical emphases on personal decision, power encounter, and healing swept me into their orbit.

It has been a long journey, but along the way I left the Lutheran Church behind. Calvary Chapel, too. I even got a permanent haircut. In time I came to swim in the mainstream of evangelicalism. Soul-winning, hard-hitting sermons, and revival hymns became staples of my diet. But deep inside I knew that something was terribly wrong. Something was missing. My friends bravely proclaimed the certainty of evangelical theology, but somewhere the mystery of God was lost.

I realize that not all evangelical churches are the same. And I have been many places where the profundity of spiritual life and the holy character of worship are celebrated. These are places where the sermon is secondary to a holy encounter with God. Nevertheless, I have a theory: I suspect that there is a growing dissatisfaction in many evangelical churches today. Many people—myself included—are looking for a place where the dignity of tradition and ritual, the power of the charismatic renewal, and the Word-centered theology of evangelicalism come together. And nowhere is this longing felt more deeply than in the context of worship.

What Happens When Christians Worship?

Perhaps these migrations among my friends and students have forced me to ask new questions about what we are doing when we worship.

In our zeal to be practical and relevant, perhaps we have missed something. We are participatory—including testimonies and prayers and choruses from the congregation—and yet some are saying that their experiences seem hollow. *They are not really participating.* We engineer "worship experiences," and yet heartfelt needs seem still to go wanting.

So what is true worship? Worship, I believe, is a *divine encounter* that touches many dimensions of my personhood. It is an encounter in which God's glory and word and grace are unveiled, and we respond, in songs and prayers of celebration. Worshippers seek an encounter with the glory of God, his transcendent power, his supernatural mystery— and in so doing, recognize a Lord whose majesty evokes strong praise, petition, and transformation.

But my own Christian training has emptied Sunday's eleven o'clock hour of almost all of God's majesty and mystery. Divine encounters seem few. Why?

I believe there are two reasons. First, we have been taught that the sermon must exposit the biblical texts and that immediate and timely application should follow every message. While all of this is true, nothing has been left to our imaginations. Little has been left for our hearts to ponder—except post-sermon feelings of conviction and exhortation. We leave the church hour thinking more about what we must do than wondering about the mystery of God and his doings on our behalf. Therefore we have created a worship experience that is at best intellectual—a worship that studies the Bible. Homilies have evolved into thirty-minute teaching sessions. And even when these teaching sessions do touch our emotions, too often it is only to convict us of wrongdoing and inadequacy.

> *We leave the church hour thinking more about what we must do than wondering about the mystery of God and his doings on our behalf.*

To reinforce this "teaching" approach to worship, we have created our own liturgy, and its rhythm goes like this: Sing, pray, sing, pray, preach, pray, sing, pray, and leave. Before long the monotony of such a cadence can leave us numb, wondering if there is no new form, no new dance that can be written for us. Even benedictions have become nothing more than reminders of the sermon's three points. These observations have forced me to wonder what is really happening when Christians today "worship." It has forced me to question our role as worship leaders, the function of the sanctuary, the aesthetics of our music, and the content of our prayers.

But there is a second problem that gets in our way. In Romans 12:1, Paul suggests that worship must involve the everyday affairs of living. He says, "Offer your bodies as living sacrifices, holy and pleasing to God—this is your spiritual act of worship." While it is true that worship should be an ongoing moment-to-moment expression of our love for God, I believe that this perspective can also distort the deeper value of worship in the church. Rather than encountering God, our worship has become *ethical.*

Good Christian behavior has become the expression of true, spiritual worship. The Sunday church hour has become an equipping/training station for our lives. Rather than being an "other-worldly" encounter reminding us of our heavenly identity, it has become "worldly" in the sense that its focus is wholly horizontal, sharpening our discipleship in the world, but failing to bring us face to face with God.

I see this problem illustrated symbolically in our use of the sacraments. In what sense is the Lord's Supper a unique meal with Christ? What has become of the church's historic interest in "divine presence" when serving these elements? Does this meal emphasize fellowship and confession with others, or does it represent communion and an encounter with God? I see liturgical routines that emphasize this "horizontal" theology, routines that gradually shape worshippers to miss God altogether. Such worshippers never come to know Eucharist-as-encounter.

I recently attended an independent, charismatic church in England for a number of months where the zeal for worship was known throughout the city. Curiously, the Lord's Supper was not celebrated in corporate worship. Instead, a folding table with a chalice and a plate of bread was set up at the back of the sanctuary for members to use as they saw fit.

"And how do they use it?" I asked the pastor.

"Most use it for reconciliation," he said. When two people are reconciled from a division, they may walk to the table and confirm their new unity by taking the bread. It was only after a long discussion over lunch that the pastor courageously agreed that the elders of the church had to rethink their theology about this.

The same is true with baptism. Remarkably, infant baptisms and dedications become platforms for talking about better parenting. Rather than providing an opportunity to see in the child a living icon of our own spiritual vulnerability and God's graciousness, the baptismal font has become a platform, a pulpit for another sermon. I have actually left such baptism services despairing over being an inadequate parent rather than contemplating the wonder of my childlike dependence on the generous mercy of God.

Thus, two handicaps stand in our way. We have reduced our worship service to intellectual exhortations and ethical behavior. Don't misunderstand me. Both of these are good. But by themselves, these things can't evoke the sort of divine encounter so many of us yearn to find when we meet together on Sunday morning.

Mystery and the Supernatural

I believe that Christians are yearning to recapture worship that lifts us—as a medieval cathedral lifted the eyes of the fourteenth-century worshipper—to truly meet God, to truly worship. Some will object, however, saying that such an attitude is gnostic ("such world-denying behavior!") or narcissistic ("such emphasis on personal gratification!"). But it is neither of these. Incarnational theology demands that our worship should emphasize "encountering God." The mystery of our faith comes alive in the eruption of God's divine presence in the commonplace things of life. But if it is only the commonplace that we see, we may fail ever to see God at all.

And so I ask, How can this seeing happen? What will facilitate this eruption of divine encounters for me as I worship? And I wonder about a tougher question: *Can the Western church find merit in something that is neither intellectual nor ethical?*

For a number of years I served on the staff of a Presbyterian church in Illinois. Among my many excellent memories, worship stands out. Its splendor had to do with many things: the architecture of the building (towering stained glass that paraded the heroes of the Bible; woodcarvings of angels and saints adorning wall and pillar); the music (instruments, organ, voice); the dignity of its liturgists (their dress, speech, and demeanor); theologically informed liturgies (crafting space for confession, silence, Word, and response alike); and the attitudes of the congregation (expectant, responsive, hushed as worship unfolded). Even our lighting was intentional, aimed at enhancing visual stimuli that would direct men and women to God. Our organist worked hard to build artful transitions between events in the worship service.

I recall sitting in the sanctuary next to our (then) nine-year-old daughter. Each Sunday we would pick a window and tell the story of who was represented there and what the symbols meant. They were beautiful and powerful and instructive. And they were densely theological, using our eyes as vehicles for inspiration. The effect was disarming when one Sunday I asked her to stand and turn to count how many "stained-glass" people were watching us in the pew. She realized we were surrounded by a "host of witnesses" who had been faithful to God despite their circumstances (Hebrews 12:1). On another Sunday our talk of a window was interrupted by bells. The bell choir had surrounded the sanctuary and from every wall, complex and delightful notes swelled in volume, calling us to worship. It was unworldly—even heavenly.

I tell this story to suggest that many worshippers come looking for more than fellowship, exposition and exhortation. They seek an experience of "the holy." They come looking for awe and reverence, mystery and transcendence. For this to happen, all of their sensory faculties need to be engaged: Their sense of sight, sound, touch, and smell are powerful avenues of communication. One glance at the Old Testament directions for orchestrating Temple worship will remove all doubt that this is our task. Fire, incense, tapestry and gold joined with ritual activities that reminded worshippers of the reverential awe demanded of them. Bells and breastplates provided a visual feast, evoking images of God's presence. Even the Temple's architecture did this. One climbed higher as steps led "up" to the Holy Place.

> **M**any worshippers come looking for more than fellowship, exposition and exhortation. They seek an experience of "the holy."

Therefore, modern Christian worshippers need to reclaim their Old Testament heritage. We need to unburden ourselves of those reflexes forged during the Reformation and Enlightenment that shunned the pageantry and visual media of medieval Catholicism. But as we head down this road, we must hear a warning that speaks to us out of the centuries. Spiritual transcendence does not occur simply through aesthetic techniques. Bells and glass and pageantry will not in themselves bring the spiritual reality we seek. Mysticism is not a magic act. It is an outgrowth of a genuine and vibrant relationship with God. Gourmet recipes should always be served on expensive china; but exquisite china in itself can never supply a meal.

I recall attending vespers at one of the most beautiful chapels in the world in one of Cambridge University's many colleges. The architecture, the choir, the liturgy—every aspect of the experience was overwhelmingly beautiful. And yet something dreadful occurred to me before it was over. Almost no one was in attendance. This worship did not seem to be linked to a richly growing spiritual life. At least from my vantage, few saw this as a place of spiritual nourishment.

The Pastor as Priest

My evangelical roots have reminded me in no uncertain terms that the pastor is "one" with the people. I uphold Luther's "priesthood of all believers." In Presbyterian parlance the pastor is one of the elders—a teaching elder—alongside so many other elders. And I believe that is right and good.

However, this belief has also produced some unfortunate effects among leaders in the church. Our demeanor, our dress, our participatory leadership style have evolved to communicate that there is no hierarchy in our congregations. I do not agree with this approach to church leadership, especially as it relates to worship.

Don't misunderstand me. I'm not suggesting that pastors have privileges in the grace of God or the economy of the church unavailable to others. But I am suggesting that in worship, the pastor must become priest. *The pastor plays a significant role in the divine encounter offered in worship.* The pastor assumes the role of mediator, incarnating God to the people, forging an atmosphere and image that men and women will absorb when they contemplate divine things. When I come to my kitchen hungry, I often take the food that is most easily within reach. When we come to worship empty, we assimilate those images that are most accessible. I have seen this at work again and again. One pastor I have watched is serious and severe. One seems to be "going through the motions." Another exudes grace radiantly and powerfully. As they conduct worship, they set patterns in place that form the image of God in worshippers' minds.

I remember when one of our daughters was baptized. She stood near the baptismal font as our pastor bent over asking her questions of faith. His dignity, his well-prepared words, his touch and his gaze all entered the archive of her experience. Later she said, "I remember Pastor coming near and I was covered and lost in his long black robes and he baptized me." Responses from a standing congregation and a thundering hymn cemented images that have never gone away.

If it is true that we are priests and mediators of God's encounter with his people, then we must be intentional about everything we do as worship leaders. We must be architects of worship because it is through our craft that we will be able to enrich and build the spiritual lives of our people. Through our craft, we will facilitate worship. In most Christian traditions we are comfortable saying that a pastor's words must be found true because as we preach we speak for God. But, really, more than that is required for true leadership in the church. As worship

> *If it is true that we are priests and mediators of God's encounter with his people, then we must be intentional about everything we do as worship leaders.*

leaders, our complete conduct must be true because, like it or not, all that we do speaks volumes about God and his desires.

There are no gimmicks that can take the place of this kind of genuine leadership in worship. Priestly leadership is not a set of learned theatrical skills. As pastor-priest we bring to the congregation the glory of *our* encounter with God. Having spent long, enduring time in the Lord's presence, we speak to our congregations *out of those encounters.* And as I think carefully how I translate the elements of this encounter to my people, I create forms which express where I have been. A friend described to me his experience worshipping at All Soul's Church in London when John Stott was preaching. For the entire service up to the sermon, Stott was on his knees in prayer. And then when he spoke he brought to his leadership the freshness of being in God's presence.

Recitation and Ritual

True worship must facilitate a divine encounter. It must evoke deeper mysteries. It must lift us. And as we worship, liturgists and leaders must become a priesthood, leading people to God, showing the depth of their own experiences, reflecting his glory, pointing weary souls heavenward.

But I think there is another element to a true worship experience that cannot be missed. Many modern Christian traditions have taught us to champion spontaneity and to make a virtue out of informality. Some of us are sure that God cannot hear formally written prayers. Corporately spoken creeds, prayers, and liturgies serve only to stifle us and the Lord, or so the argument goes.

But I do not believe this is true. Of course, there are liturgies that are memorized and meaningless, words that congregations follow mindlessly every week. But there can be great meaning and worship evoked through planned, repetitive speech-forms that accompany every service. That is, when I introduce worship, when I offer the Eucharist, when I baptize, even when I bury, I can employ familiar, dignified forms that evoke a history and an importance among my listeners. I reflect, for instance, on why both the marginally-churched and the faithful Christian want to hear Psalm 23 recited at a funeral, and 1 Corinthians 13 at a wedding, and the hymn "Amazing Grace" at thresholds of crisis. There is something reassuring in this recitation of old things, something that links us in continuity with history and tradition. It is like holding a book well-worn by your grandparent's fingers. In some mysterious way, we feel strengthened.

> *There is something reassuring in this recitation of old things, something that links us in continuity with history and tradition. It is like holding a book well-worn by your grandparent's fingers. In some mysterious way, we feel strengthened.*

I recall a pastor in Chicago who created his own liturgy for every infant baptism. He would hold the child aloft and introduce him or her to the congregation, saying (in various ways), "This is your new family." But then he would begin to recite an artful, dignified paragraph—a rich, full-bodied piece—about this child's vulnerability and God's love. He spoke about how God loves us before we are even able to know him, before we can see beyond our own fingers. He recited this verbatim for every baptism, and each time it sounded as if it was his first time. Imagine the wedding of imagery and theology here! People looked forward to these baptisms, for they spoke not just of cute babies, but of us as well. In the child we could see our vulnerability and our near-sightedness and God's redeeming, forgiving love.

The same is true for benedictions. Recitation is a reminder of what is profound and important. Recitation assures us that we are where we should be. Recitation carries us with familiarity when sometimes we cannot carry ourselves.

How often baptisms become opportunities to chat about kids and parents! How often benedictions become one more chance to reinforce the sermon!

I started a tradition in one of my theology classes that now won't die. I learned that our students had never heard of Israel's great *Shema Isra'el* in Deuteronomy 6. So we began reciting it in Hebrew at the start of each class period. At first they thought it was odd. Then they knew that they had inherited it. And then they wouldn't let me begin class without it. Was it novelty? Not by the twelfth week. It set the rhythm, it moored us theologically, and it centered us in a tradition as old as Moses.

I also see it on the faces of students when I lead them on trips to Israel. When we stand near the Sea of Galilee and recite the Beatitudes near where Jesus said them, I am *anchoring* them. I am giving them a treasure—a gift of vision and sound to which they may turn in memory for many years. I also prepare them in advance. Perhaps I will have them memorize the Twenty-Third Psalm and then hold it in abeyance until they enter the desert, only there to recite it alone as biblical shepherds often did. To sit in the desert, to feel the jeopardy of a sheep in the wilderness, and to recite an ancient hymn of God's provision is to cultivate a divine encounter that will remain for life.

Therefore, my plea is for worship that becomes familiar but not trite, that employs dignified language but is not stilted, and language that is planned but is not mechanical.

As a child I grew up in a Lutheran tradition that still stays with me today. After forty years I can recall the melodies of the liturgies, the cadence of the Nicene Creed, even portions of the set Eucharistic prayers. When I have little else to fall back on, these deep-set foundations become my security. I believe all worshippers need to build immovable foundations like these.

God-Centered Worship

All of this—worship that is a divine encounter, pastors with priestly skills, language that is liturgically rich—means that we build a service that is theocentric rather than centered on the human community. This sort of worship doesn't merely tell people about God, it invites them to meet God, to engage him in his presence. This worship makes us less aware of the people sitting nearby and more aware of God who is above. In addition, this worship is creative as it permits men, women and children to employ numerous avenues of expression—from creative use of sound to expressive uses of color and movement. But in each of these expressions, the aim is never to entertain or inspire the congregation. The aim is to worship God with abandon—the kind of worship that solicits no spectators.

Perhaps I think about this most clearly when I consider the relationship between the choir and its congregation. To what extent does the choir sing *for the congregation*, placing worshippers into the role of audience? To what extent is the choir's service a *horizontal* work that finds approval only when it satisfies the human ear? Consider even the geography of our sanctuaries and how architecture defines that relationship. After all, doesn't the choir face the congregation? How can a choir truly facilitate divine worship?

I also think of the function of the pastoral prayer. These are horizontal works, too, whenever they lapse into teaching ("Lord, we thank you that you sent your Son to die for us on the cross"), preaching ("Lord, help us to follow you in the following three ways"), or counseling ("Lord, we know that you heal us when we turn from our sins").

Sometimes I have wondered what new Christians must think when someone announces, "Let us pray," and then continues to talk horizontally to the congregation ("Now with your eyes closed, I want you to consider what God might be saying"). I once knew a pastor who led the pastoral prayer actually looking at the congregation as if he were preaching. All of these liturgical decisions are signals to the congregation about what it is we think we are doing when we worship.

But it does not need to be this way. My students and colleagues are looking for worship that weds dignity and spontaneity, worship that is theologically informed and liturgically intentional. My students and friends are migrating, looking for pastors who can be priests, liturgists who can evoke divine encounters, worship services that do not push them into the world to merely be better Christians, but rather draw them into a divine refuge—a divine encounter that lifts their lives and souls to an entirely new plateau.

Chapter 4
Contemporary Worship:
What Does Worship From the Heart Look Like?

by KIM HILL with
LISA HARPER

Last year my husband, Rob, and I flew from Nashville to North Carolina to watch a college basketball game between Duke University and The University of North Carolina. Rob went to graduate school at Duke and is a sports fanatic, so he was really excited that we were actually going to be in the stands at one of the most hotly contested collegiate ballgames of the year. I confess that I wasn't nearly as enthusiastic about the game as he was, especially after we paid a scalper nearly as much as our mortgage payment for the tickets!

When we finally made it to our seats, I found myself more interested in watching the fans than the game. People of every shape, size, color, and background were cheering wildly for their respective team. Although it was cold, a lot of male students were bare-chested with slogans painted all over their upper bodies in blue. Hundreds of fans had team logos painted on their faces.

I was mesmerized by a huge group of students from Duke's graduate school who were chanting and jumping up and down in unison. They were so frenzied and passionate, as if they were performing some sort of sacred ritual. They were utterly and completely devoted to this game where the object is to throw a leather ball into a hoop more often than your opponent. I soon realized the reason I was transfixed by their demonstration of devotion was because it was a startling experience of *déjà vu*.

I had witnessed that very same passionate fervency at a women's worship conference the previous weekend in California. I had spent the better part of twenty-four hours in a room with over a thousand women who were passionately devoted to the Lord. They also cheered and sang and swayed in unison as they demonstrated their love for Christ with heartfelt adoration and abandon. It hit me like a ton of bricks that these brilliant, young, successful, soon-to-be doctors and lawyers were *worshipping*…very much like my friends in Los Angeles. They just weren't worshipping God.

> I *didn't want to explain why I was so emotional about a bunch of men running around in shorts.*

I found myself crying while throngs of Duke fans cheered all around me. Thankfully, Rob was so engrossed in the game that he didn't notice my tears; I didn't want to ruin his experience or try to explain why I was so emotional about a bunch of men running around in shorts. I told him later that night that I was crying over the fact that most of us don't even recognize when we worship things other than our Creator. Like the Israelites, we kneel in front of "golden calves" that divert our attention from the only true God. I'm not a "sports-Scrooge." I enjoy athletics and think sports are a great aspect of life. However, they pale next to the King of Kings and Lord of Lords—everything pales next to him.

Worshipping from the heart involves focusing all of our attention and affection on one thing. The result of ardent, disciplined focus is adoration, which should be reserved for God alone. In addition, this singular focus leads to passion, commitment, and devotion, which first must be spent on the "Lord God Almighty, who was. and is, and is to come."

The prophet Isaiah talks about removing the stones before we can worship the Lord. I think the stones represent anything that gets in the way of giving the Lord the first fruits of our attention and affection. College basketball is just one of many substitutes in our culture that distract us from worshipping the Lord with all our hearts. We live in a post-modern culture that not only considers Judeo-Christian principles antiquated, but also hyperactively bombards us with countless things that compete for our attention and siphon off our divine affections.

Last week between changing Benjamin's diapers, driving Graham to and from basketball camp, arranging flights to a weekend concert, and juggling day-to-day responsibilities, I'd had a hard time focusing on the Lord. In fact, as I drove and talked to my travel agent on the phone, I had a hard time focusing on the road, much less focusing on the Lord. Thousands of people, just like me, are trying to juggle families and jobs and manage their homes. Most of us are so distracted by responsibilities and relationships that we rarely focus all of our attention on the Lord. The first fruits of our affection are diluted by the minutiae of life.

Richard Foster writes, "Today the heart of God is an open wound of love. He aches over our distance and preoccupation. He mourns that we do not draw near to Him. He grieves that we have forgotten Him. He weeps over our obsession with muchness and manyness. He longs for our presence." [1]

*"Turn your eyes upon Jesus,
Look full in His wonderful
  face.
And the things of earth will
  grow strangely dim
In the light of His glory and
  grace."*
—Helen H. Lemmel

I'm beginning to understand that God aches over my distance and preoccupation. I'm learning to carve out time for a daily "Sabbath," when I rest in the knowledge of God's mercy and his character. It's not the stereotypical quiet time, and it's not a time for Bible study either—it's a time to be still...absolutely still. Without stillness, in which God reminds me that he alone is worthy of my adoration, my heart is like a three-legged stool, much too wobbly for worship. When I give my heavenly Father undivided attention, my heart is made steadfast and warmed by his nearness.

The Posture of a Worshipping Heart

Most people assume that since I've been a contemporary Christian recording artist for well over a decade, worship is second nature to me. But it's been a long road full of dead ends and wrong turns. I've had the opportunity to sing Christian music all over the world, but I've only recently learned what it means to *lead* worship.

*My little brother Jamie
and I would sing and
dance and pass around
a hat for coins!*

When I was a little girl in Mississippi, I knew exactly what I wanted to be when I grew up. My schoolmates changed their career aspirations from year to year—one year they wanted to be firefighters, the next year they wanted to be astronauts. My aspiration never wavered. I've wanted to be a singer for as long as I can remember. When I was in the first grade, I dreamed of being on stage.

I sang constantly and used to perform for anyone who would listen. We always had a lot of people coming and going at our house. My little brother Jamie and I would sing and dance and pass around a hat for coins! One of my favorite routines was to hide behind a big chair in the living room and sing Elvis songs, while Jamie danced and lip-synced for the "audience."

Granddaddy Hill, who lived near us in Mississippi, loved the fact that I was such a ham. "Kim, one of these days I'm going to take you up to Nashville and make you a big country star," he told me.

Wide-eyed, I asked, "Do you really know anybody in Nashville, Paw-Paw?"

Gruffly he replied, "I think I know a few people up there, and as soon as they hear you sing, they'll have you on the Grand Ole Opry!"

Granddaddy was a big talker—he could sell ice in Iceland. I believed wholeheartedly I was going to sing in Nashville when I grew up.

When I was in fourth grade, Mom gave me her old Sears Silvertone, $19.99 guitar. I guess she decided that I was serious enough about music to start taking lessons. My first and only guitar lessons took place in the Pigford Building in downtown Meridian, Mississippi. It was a musty, dark old building, but my guitar teacher, Carl, was on the colorful side.

Carl first taught me songs by Hank Williams Sr., insisting, "It's important to know the country standards, so I'm going to teach you the best county songs ever written." I learned Williams' "I'm So Lonesome I Could Cry" and other country classics. I walked around the house singing mournful tunes about unrequited love that my parents didn't like. Carl's country repertoire didn't quite fit their musical tastes.

After six weeks of lessons in the Pigford Building, Mom and Dad had a talk with me. Mom sat me down and said, "Kim, we think you've learned enough about the guitar to start playing from songbooks, and if you're going to walk around singing all the time, we'd rather you sing music that we like." So they bought me a songbook of 1970s' hits in addition to Jim Croce and Helen Reddy songbooks. Pretty soon I was walking around the house belting out, "I am woman, hear me roar in numbers too big to ignore…"!

Then a miracle happened in our family. Dad found out that he needed surgery to remove polyps on his vocal chords. The doctors warned that the polyps might be cancerous. Mom and Dad were really scared. Mom took a Bible her father had given her to the hospital to read. Mom and Dad attended church, but had never really read the Bible. Mom read the book of John the night before Dad's surgery and realized that she didn't know the Lord. She prayed the sinner's prayer by herself in the hospital that night and committed her life to Jesus Christ. Following the surgery (the polyps weren't cancerous), Dad also had a significant spiritual experience and recommitted his life to Christ.

Immediately, I noticed a change in my parents' lives. No longer were they hosting parties with live music and beer; instead people were coming over to study the Bible and pray.

Finally, I said, "Mama, what happened to you and Daddy? Why are people coming over to our house and talking about Jesus?"

"Kim, your Dad and I have become Christians," Mama replied.

"I thought we already were Christians, Mama. We go to church every Sunday."

"Sweetheart, there's a lot more to being a Christian than just going to church. There's a big difference between being religious and having a relationship with Jesus Christ."

Mom was prepared for the day when I would ask her about the Lord. She had bought a glove with multicolored fingers from the Baptist bookstore that was used as a tool to explain the gospel to children. She went into her room, got the glove, and then using each finger explained sin, repentance, and the gospel of grace to me.

Mom gently took my hand, and we knelt down beside her bed and prayed together.

"Kim, do you understand why Jesus had to come and die on the cross?" I told her that I understood. She asked if I would like to ask Jesus to come into my heart and save me from my sins.

"Yes, Mama, I want to ask Jesus to come into my heart," I said. Mom gently took my hand, and we knelt down beside her bed and prayed together. It was such a sweet blessing to be introduced to Jesus Christ by my mom.

Soon the type of music we sang changed as well as "Who" we were singing to. Praise music filled our home. Mom drove us to school every day in her red convertible singing "This Is the Day." And then my parents made a deal with me: As long as I didn't listen to secular music on the radio, they would buy me any Christian music I wanted. The genre called contemporary Christian music was brand new, and I bought every Christian eight track available. I decided that I wasn't going to be just a singer, but I was going to be a Christian singer…and I was.

Within months of moving to Nashville after college, I signed a recording contract. It was exciting to be using my musical talent to minister God's love to others. I felt that I was doing exactly what God created me to do. The first couple of years as a "professional Christian artist" were wonderful. I sang about his love and then shared the gospel with hundreds of fans after most concerts. In no time, it seemed, I had five number-one singles and was on an eighty-city, sold-out tour with Amy Grant. My picture was on magazine covers, and my music was played on radio stations all over the world. But, unfortunately, I didn't feel that worshipping the Lord was the first priority of my career anymore.

Back then, "worship" music didn't sell records. So the only time I felt as if I was really leading others in worship was at the *end* of a sixty- or ninety-minute concert. The band would leave the stage, and I would sing "Jesus, What a Wonder You Are" with just my guitar. Those moments became precious, holy times…always my favorite part of each concert.

It took several years of personal and professional disappointment and disillusionment for God to teach me how to worship throughout the "whole concert." I had lost sight of the fact that God had called and gifted me for *his purpose.* I was supposed to be making *his name* great among the people, not my own. God made this crystal clear during a Bible class I took through a ministry in Nashville. We had a guest speaker who cut several singers' hearts to the quick with his insightful views on the Christian music "industry." Rick Joyner, a popular Bible teacher and author of *Mobilizing the Army of God,* writes:

> The first step toward repentance is to return to our first love—worshipping him. Because all music promotes worship in some form, if our hearts are not right we will pervert the power of his anointing. Our music must promote the worship of the Father, obedience to the Spirit and the witness of Jesus. If the Christian music establishment does not repent, and return to its first love, its lamp stand will soon be removed and what light it now has will go out. When we do repent, we will find the greatest desire of our heart, peace, and even greater resources for the extravagant worship of the King.[2]

God stripped away everything I'd placed my hope in—recognition, relationships, and riches—until I returned to my first love, worshipping him. He revealed to me that I had "medicated" myself with stuff and people to numb my desire to be loved perfectly—a desire that only our

Abba, Father, can fill. The longing that God restored in my heart for his presence spread over into every aspect of life, including my career. I remembered that I was created to do more than perform, entertain, and sell records. I wanted to sing songs that pointed others to the wonder of our heavenly Father. I wanted to use whatever talent I had to help lead others into his presence. I wanted to use music to grab others by the hand and heart and to walk with them to God's throne of grace. If that meant singing to a few people in a small church, then that was OK by me. If it meant simply teaching my little boys about the character of God when I sang them to sleep at night, then that was OK, too.

Perfect Posture Comes From Proper Perspective

Brokenness was the key to my spiritual renewal in the area of worship. Once I began to magnify God's greatness, my smallness was apparent; as I praised his strength, my weaknesses were illuminated. We must have a proper perspective of our neediness against the backdrop of God's grace. Our hearts will never be fully engaged in worship until we humbly acknowledge our frail humanity and God's deity. Our hearts will be free to worship God only when our hearts have been broken by the miracle of his gospel. To focus all of our attention and affection on One is to recognize God as our rescuer and redeemer.

About a year ago, one of the most powerful worship experiences I've ever had occurred at home in my office. My office is on the lower level of our home, so I'm never too far from our boys' shrieks of laughter or the nanny's shriek of terror over the latest fake snake or insect they delight in tormenting her with.

On this particular morning, I had retreated to my office not to work on the computer or send a fax, but to cry. I was so overwhelmed with the pressures of being a mom, wife, daughter, sister, friend, and working woman that I thought I would snap. I felt as if I was failing

"God, You've kept track of my every toss and turn through the sleepless nights, each tear entered in Your ledger, each ache written in Your book."
—Psalm 56:8
(The Message)

at everything! I was impatient with the kids and really mad at my husband. I had dropped the ball in several key business situations. I was so exasperated with my own ineptitude that if someone had introduced me to the kind, submissive, domestic, "Proverbs 31" woman, I probably would've punched her!

I lay on the floor in my office and sobbed, hoping the boys wouldn't come bounding downstairs to show me their latest discovery. I wept over my harsh words and hard heart. I prayed and asked God to help me. My words weren't polished or profound. Basically, I just cried out for him to rescue me and redeem the ugly things I'd said and done. I told God that I was desperate for his comfort and peace. Then I started singing because I usually sing (or eat chocolate) when I'm upset. Those simple praise choruses became winged prayers that flew right to the heart of God. He ministered to me in tangible, profound ways that morning. God heard my cries; he became my "balm of Gilead." My heaviest tears resulted in my richest worship.

I had the privilege of visiting Israel last year and was deeply affected by the reverence that religious Jews have for God. Our tour bus arrived in Jerusalem on a Friday afternoon. My friend Lisa and I decided to go for a run because we needed to get some fresh air and exercise after the torture of being tourists! We threw on some running tights and T-shirts and jogged out of our hotel, gleeful to have a few minutes of freedom. We didn't realize we were running on the Jewish Sabbath until we rounded a corner and almost ran smack into some Hasidic Jewish men complete with long black coats, curly side burns, and hats. They were walking to the synagogue nearby (one of the most famous in the world) and were obviously not pleased by our presence or apparel. Lisa and I soon found ourselves right in the middle of a Sabbath-celebrating pedestrian traffic jam. We were at once embarrassed by our lack of respect for their culture and quickly found a side road to make a hasty retreat.

Although they do not recognize Jesus Christ as the Messiah, most of the Jews we met in Israel have more reverence and passion for Jehovah than most Christians I know. On the Jewish Sabbath, they say this prayer: "Our hearts are restless all week, until today they rest again in Thee." They have learned to take a break from the distractions in their world and humbly acknowledge that God is the ruler over everything, including their lives.

Like those sincere Jewish men and women, we must learn to humble ourselves in order "to grasp how wide and long and high and deep is the love" that the Father has for us. We must acknowledge the fact that we're crippled...we're crippled by sin, our hearts are deformed by pride, and God's word tells us that there is nothing righteous in us. But if we put our trust in Christ, our sins have been covered by the blood of God's Son. He will rescue us from barren places and give us a seat at his banquet table. Our hearts should be overwhelmed by the miracle of the gospel. We should be amazed that God loves us because of his character instead of our performance, or lack thereof. We should shout with joy over the fact that

> "*As we discover and experience the majesty of God, the reality of His presence in our lives, and His availability to us in our times of need, we will be unable to keep from worshipping Him. It's a natural response."*
> —*John Wimber*

while we were still sinners, God loved us. Gratitude for his grace is what softens our hearts and bends them before the Lord in the posture of worship.

The word *worship* was actually shortened from the Old English word *worthship*. *Worthship* was primarily used to describe people's acknowledgement of the supreme worth of God. Before we can worship God with all our hearts, we must first acknowledge his worthiness. We must think rightly about God. We must consider the attributes of a King, who not only created the universe, but who also rescues cripples and redeems the unworthy. Heartfelt worship takes place when sinners recognize the cost of their salvation and the worth of their Savior.

The Extravagance of Heartfelt Worship

One of the silliest things I do when my husband is out of town is dance by myself through our house. Once in a while, after I've put the kids to bed, I'll put a favorite CD on the stereo and dance all over the house with reckless abandon. I especially love to wiggle in my socks because then I can incorporate sliding on the hardwood floors into my dance routine! I usually end up collapsing on the couch in self-conscious laughter, wondering if the neighbors were able to see me through the blinds! But for a few precious moments, I'm not self-conscious, I'm completely uninhibited.

My nighttime solo dancing is probably one of the reasons that I love the story of David dancing before the Lord with reckless abandon. I can just picture the king of Israel in a linen sheath, leaping before his Father with a heart full of thanksgiving. David is a beautiful example of extravagant worship. His wife is an ugly portrait of someone whose insecurity and self-consciousness bind her heart with cords of criticism and discontentment.

> When those who were carrying the ark of the Lord had taken six steps, he sacrificed a bull and a fattened calf. David, wearing a linen ephod, danced before the Lord with all his might, while he and the entire house of Israel brought up the ark of the Lord with

shouts and the sound of trumpets. As the ark of the Lord was entering the City of David, Michal daughter of Saul watched from a window. And when she saw King David leaping and dancing before the Lord, she despised him in her heart. When David returned home to bless his household, Michal daughter of Saul came out to meet him and said, "How the king of Israel has distinguished himself today, disrobing in the sight of the slave girls of his servants, as any vulgar fellow would!" David said to Michal, "It was before the Lord, who chose me rather than your father or anyone from his house when he appointed me ruler over the Lord's people Israel—I will celebrate before the Lord. I will become even more undignified than this, and I will be humiliated in my own eyes.

—2 Samuel 6:13-16, 20-22a

I want to be more like King David. I want the overflow of my heart to result in extravagant worship before the Lord. Like the raucous fans at the Duke basketball game, I want to celebrate the Lord's grace and mercy with passionate abandon, whether the "blinds" of my life are open or closed.

It's been an incredible experience to lead thousands of women in worship at Renewing the Heart conferences, sponsored by Focus on the Family. Often I'll be on a platform in the middle of twenty thousand women singing praises to the Lord. (Sometimes I'm tempted to dance before God as David did, but wearing a skirt and heels limits my leaping!) It's been amazing to watch the women's responses to authentic praise and worship. Most of the conference attendants come from conservative church backgrounds where demonstrative worship is not appropriate. But when they sit in the safety and anonymity of a public arena filled with thousands of others who are singing praises to the Lord, their inhibitions fade.

"Then the temple of the Lord was filled with a cloud, and the priests could not perform their service because of the cloud, for the glory of the Lord filled the temple of God."
—*2 Chronicles 5:13b-14*

Those who began with taut faces that registered disapproval, soon begin to loosen up. Within a few hours, the "Michals" among us begin weeping and raising their hands—perhaps for the first time—as they sing to the Lord. And their heartfelt adoration seems to hasten God's presence. Their countenances change as they begin to experience *extravagant* worship. As I watch the women's faces begin to glow in the rapture of worship, I am reminded of Peter at Jesus' transfiguration.

I've received hundreds of letters and e-mails from women touched by the Lord through the music. Several women have told me that they prayed to commit their lives to Christ after experiencing God's presence through worship. The glory of the Lord fills the temple of their hearts just as it's recorded in 2 Chronicles.

I've worked for many pastors and Christian leaders who have the mind-set that music is just "fluff" or something to fill a few minutes of the program, while the speakers and teachers are getting prepared. Many well-meaning Christians think music should be the first thing to go when the program or worship service needs to be shortened. I actually had someone tell me that "Singers should just sing and let the speakers do the talking because music is just window dressing." I don't think God-centered worship music is ever "just window dressing." Obviously, God doesn't either, or the Levite musicians would not have stood on the east side of the altar playing cymbals, harps, and lyres, while singing, "He is good; his love endures forever."

I believe worship is the most important element in preparing hearts for the spoken word. Without worship, our hearts remain hardened soil, unprepared for the seeds planted through teaching. Any gifted speaker can manipulate or captivate an audience through carefully crafted words, but only the Holy Spirit can truly change one's heart. And I think the Holy Spirit moves more freely in hearts that have been softened and cultivated by worship.

I didn't always feel the same way about worship. I grew up in a conservative church in the South, where anything other than three hymns prior to the sermon was considered out of order. I'm quite sure if anyone had raised their hands in praise in our church, the rest of us would've thought they had chosen a very inopportune time to ask a question.

Since then I've attended several churches where demonstrative worship is the norm. While I personally enjoy worship services that are less stiff and formal, I've also been bothered by some of the emotive, experientially oriented worship found in less formal congregations. I've watched people behave as if they believed that if they clapped louder or jumped higher, the more God would be pleased. I don't believe the extremity of our physical behavior is an indication of how extravagant our worship is. Authentic worship has very little, if anything, to do with external conformity. It has everything to do with hearts that are renewed by the Holy Spirit.

Bruce Leafblad, a professor of church music and worship at Southwestern Baptist Theological Seminary in Texas, writes, "We should remember that renewal is not the same everywhere. In church history, no major renewal has ever come from forms and formats, and so it is today. The great need of the church today is neither to cling to the old or to create the new forms and formats. Our greatest need today is to recover the priority of God in our worship and in the whole of life. The crisis in worship today is not a crisis of form but of spirituality." [3]

The reason some believers still aren't experiencing true worship—even when they are active, "hand-raising" participants—is because they've only changed their outward appearance. It's so much easier to make external changes in our

> "*Yet a time is coming and has now come when the true worshipers will worship the Father in spirit and truth, for they are the kind of worshipers the Father seeks.*"—*John 4:23*

behavior than it is to have our hearts circumcised by the gospel. Only when we begin to catch a glimpse of the extravagant love it takes for a perfect God to run toward prodigals like us, will our hearts began to learn the elementary lessons of worship. We must learn to stop dancing before the altar of man's approval and to worship God solely because he is worthy of our praise. External extravagance does not necessarily please the heart of God. If we perform for others' approval when we worship God, then we're perverting the praise meant for him. The style of our worship is not what's important, the motive and intent of our heart is. The extravagance of our worship is meant for an audience of One.

New Worship: Participation Replaces Performance

I was at a dinner recently with several sales representatives for the Christian music industry. They asked me what I'd been doing creatively, and I told them how excited I was to be leading worship at women's conferences. I went on to explain that I thought the main reason God had called me back into the arena of contemporary Christian music was to help our industry return to worship as our primary focus.

One representative told me that he hated to see so many artists jump on the "worship bandwagon" for purely commercial reasons. He lamented the fact that worship was once again becoming popular and even financially viable within the recording industry. He was sure the marketplace would pervert the purity of it.

Although I agree with many of his concerns, I'm thankful that "worship music" is enjoying a renaissance. Worship is everywhere: Mainline churches are incorporating contemporary worship into their services; worship-oriented bands like Delirious? (a great group from England) are selling out concerts and getting the attention of the secular media; radio stations are including worship music in their regular programming formats; worship songs are topping contemporary Christian music radio charts; and worship-oriented record labels are popping up all over Nashville.

It's interesting to note that, once again, young people are leading the way in this righteous revolution, just as they did during the Jesus movement of the sixties. Sally Morgenthaler, founder of Worship Evangelism Concepts, writes effectively about this trend:

> Music has the ability to access the human soul faster than anything else. Our whole society—especially those younger than thirty—craves the "medicine" of music. The percentage of income spent on tapes and CDs has risen dramatically in the last decade. When we apply this trend to the intense spiritual searching that's a fact of life as we round the bend of the next millennium, it shouldn't surprise us that God is harnessing music to tell people he loves them. God is an efficient God and will use the most effective means in any culture to reach the lost.[4]

Robert Webber, Director of the Institute for Worship Studies and Professor of Theology at Wheaton College, expounds on the desire for participatory worship in our postmodern culture: "Remember that communication in a postmodern world has shifted from verbal explanation to immersed participation in events. The key to good worship is to stay away from entertainment models and return worship to the people. This generation wants to participate."[5]

Webber adds, "This generation wants an authentic embodiment of worship—and young people are quick and can spot a phony a mile away. But when worship is genuine and done *by* them—not to them or for them—they will respond."[6]

I'm certainly no expert on statistics and cultural trends, but I can comment on what I see now versus ten years ago at Christian concerts and conferences. People now come expecting to be engaged

Now, the most popular Christian concerts have an unplugged, participatory feel.

and to "enter-in." They want to participate instead of merely being entertained. Ten years ago, I could sing for an hour and a half, and, as long as I sang the top Christian radio hits that were familiar to the audience, most people went home satisfied they had gotten their money's worth.

Now, the most popular Christian concerts and conferences have an unplugged, participatory feel. Instead of comments about how great an artist was—or wasn't—the criteria for good events seems to be how effectively the artist engaged the crowd. I heard someone say that there's a big difference in being a performer and a "perfumer." A performer manipulates the crowd for response and approval, while a perfumer spreads the fragrance of the Lord to those within hearing—or sniffing—distance.

Even perennial top-sellers like Michael W. Smith are returning to their roots and incorporating worship sing-a-longs into their concert sets. Michael and I attend the same church in Nashville, and he recently told me that sometimes the participatory aspect of his concerts is so incredible and anointed that he ends up cutting out the rest of his solos in favor of an audience worship time. Even at our relatively conservative Presbyterian Church (PCA), the worship is evaluated weekly by our pastoral staff on the basis of whether or not it was God- and Christ-centered and on how effectively the music engaged the congregation in magnifying the Lord. Most Christians are no longer satisfied with their spectator status, but long to join in an experience of community-style worship. We long to connect with each other and our Creator.

Personally, I think there's something in us that's awakened when we worship in a crowd, large or small, of other believers. Although I love private moments of worship, something deep within my soul is touched when I'm standing shoulder to shoulder with others praising the Lord. It's as if I catch a glimpse of eternity when we kneel before the King of Kings together, crying, "Holy, Holy, Holy is the Lord God Almighty."

Heartfelt Worship: Options and Offerings

With the resurgence of worship music's popularity has come an ever-increasing list of worship styles and formats. As an artist, I'm excited to see the evolving creativity, and I applaud the diversity in the arena of worship. However, sometimes I get dizzy with the vast array of choices!

New worship formats include a return to a liturgical style of worship, which involves responsive readings, Celtic music, and silent reflection; use of the arts, incorporating drama, poetry, dance, and storytelling; and the creative use of multimedia presentations with special lighting, sound, and video graphics.

Probably because of all of the choices available, many churches and Christian events now use a "blended" worship format. Blended worship integrates the old with the new, using familiar hymns along with more contemporary praise choruses, drama, and multimedia presentations. The format helps people make the transition from a more traditional worship service to a more participatory service and lessens the potential of alienating groups within a congregation.

Women from Savannah to Seattle, from eighteen to eighty, have enthusiastically responded to the music.

We use the blended worship format at Renewing the Heart. These conferences are held across the country with ten to twenty thousand women at each event. Thus, the women represent *many* denominations, generations, and socioeconomic backgrounds, with significant cultural differences. I stand amazed, however, at how women from Savannah to Seattle, from eighteen to eighty, have enthusiastically responded to the music. Some sing loudest on the hymns (many have been rearranged to combat rote response), while others belt out the praise choruses. But almost all of them participate with a noticeable lack of restraint. They seem much more willing to sing songs that aren't in their usual repertoire if they've been able to sing a few that are! In my experience, blended formats are less intimidating and encourage participation.

I do want to emphasize, however, that form, format, and style are not the criteria to use when judging whether worship is "authentic" or not. Just like my little boys beg for a change in breakfast cereals, God's people are begging for a change in the parameters of worship. We need to quit grading worship styles, which always differ because of cultural and denominational variables and preferences. There will always be many different forms of worship for the same reason that Baskin-Robbins stays in business.

If the style of worship is biblically sound, whether it involves raising hands or responsive readings, it can be an effective vessel to offer sacrifices of praise to our heavenly Father. Richard Foster communicates this beautifully in *Streams of Living Water:*

> All of us are liturgical. That is to say, we all use material and human "forms" to express our worship of God. There simply are no non-liturgical churches. Monastics rising to recite the Night Office, Quakers waiting in silent assurance upon the Spirit, Catholics praying the rosary and revivalists sing hymns of devotion to the name of Jesus, Russian Orthodox ritualists bowing amid incense and icon and Salvation Army evangelists marching to drum and tamborine—all are engaged in liturgy. We have a choice of liturgy, but we do not have a choice of whether to use liturgy. As long as we are finite human beings, we must use liturgy; we must express ourselves through forms of worship.
>
> Liturgy, *liturgia,* simply means "the people's work." Our task in liturgy is to glorify God in the various aspects of our worship life. We are to let the reality of God shine through the human or physical forms. This is true whether we are singing hymns or burning candles, dancing in ecstatic praise or bowing in speechless adoration.[7]

Regardless of our personal worship style, our goal needs to be magnifying the Lord with all our heart. The purpose of worship is to give our hearts a language to express our adoration to the Father.

> *We need to be zealous about teaching others to "see God bigger."*

Worship allows us to look at God in such a way that we can't see anything else—especially ourselves—at the same time. Heartfelt worship enlarges our view of God to the point that he fills the entire screen of our minds. We need to be zealous about teaching others to "see God bigger" as they seek to worship him with all their heart.

I had very little experience as a worship leader when I was given the profound privilege of leading worship at Renewing the Heart conferences. There were hundreds of people in Nashville alone who were more qualified. But God typically uses weak and foolish things—broken and unqualified people—as vessels for his glory.

Thus, I've come to some conclusions in the last few years. The first is that God uses people who are desperate for his grace to lead others in worship. Vocal precision and perfection pale next to the posture of a worshipper's heart. Secondly, worship is much more than singing, dancing, reading, or any other physical manifestation. Worship is an offering of ourselves—our bodies, minds, souls, and spirits—to God. Giving him the first fruits of our attention and affection is more valuable than anything we could ever put in the offering plate on Sunday.

NOTES

1. Richard J. Foster, *Prayer: Finding the Heart's True Home*, (San Francisco, CA: Harper, 1992), 1.

2. From a lecture by Rick Joyner, The Crucible, Nashville, TN, 1996.

3. Bruce H. Leafblad, "Worship 101," Worship Leader (November/December 1998), 25.

4. Sally Morgenthaler and Robert Webber, "Youth Worship Q&A With the Experts," Youthworker (July/August 1999), 38.

5. Morgenthaler and Webber, "Youth Worship Q&A With the Experts," Youthworker

(July/August 1999), 35.

6. Morgenthaler and Webber, "Youth Worship Q&A With the Experts," Youthworker (July/August 1999), 36.

7. As quoted in Worship Leader (November/December 1998), 34.

Evangelical Worship:

A Biblical Model for the Twenty-First Century

by BRUCE H. LEAFBLAD

W hat does it mean to be an "evangelical" Christian or congregation? Given the ongoing public discussion of this question, it's
clearly better to let people decide for themselves whether "evangelical" describes their particular Christian tradition. Nevertheless, for
the purposes of this chapter, I'd like to highlight three basic qualities
that I believe all evangelical congregations share:

*An evangelical church celebrates and enacts the Evangel—the
gospel of Jesus Christ—in its worship.* Worship centers in Christ. The
good news of redemption in Christ brings rejoicing, thanksgiving,
and celebration in the "psalms, hymns and spiritual songs" of worship. Sermons declare the manifold blessings and glories of salvation.
The Lord's Table reenacts and proclaims the heart of the good news.

*An evangelical church affirms and teaches that those who are won
by the gospel are to live by the gospel.* The goal of the good news isn't

merely to provide a door of entry to heaven, but a path to maturity in Christ. Those who follow Christ will exhibit changed lives. Becoming more and more like Christ in our character, our attitudes, our values, our relationships, our way of living—this is the norm. It's by means of such personal transformation of individual lives that the church becomes salt and light in the world.

An evangelical church is committed to sharing and proclaiming the Evangel within the borders of its own community and throughout the whole world, calling all people to a personal relationship with Christ. The Great Commission is taken seriously as congregations seek to equip themselves to live out the strategy of Acts 1:8 in local, national, and international witness. Individual congregations, entire denominations, and other "sending" agencies participate in carrying out this enterprise, which is also seen to be the task of every Christian.

Even using these qualities as parameters, suggesting one worship model for all "evangelicals" is at best a risky proposition. For example, there are many congregations and even some entire denominations that describe themselves as "evangelical," yet their worship tradition consists in a fixed liturgy. For them the suggestion of some other worship pattern than their historic practice would appear presumptuous if not ludicrous. And such a suggestion is certainly not my intention.

For this reason, this chapter may have the most relevance for those evangelical churches and denominations that identify with the "free-church" tradition. Such churches are free from any fixed or predetermined worship pattern, and they're free to devise their own standard orders of worship, or even to "reinvent" their worship orders on a weekly basis if that's their pleasure. This congregational principle of local autonomy in worship has led to extensive varieties of worship practices within the evangelical, free-church tradition. It's the many free churches within the wider evangelical family that I am addressing most specifically, although I believe every tradition could profit from this examination of the biblical model for worship that follows.

The Extent of Biblical Guidance in Worship

Many of the aspects of modern worship may be traced to the biblical era and to the biblical documents themselves. However, what the Scriptures do *not* provide the church is important to note. For example, the New Testament nowhere sets forth a fixed order for Christian worship to be observed by all churches; yet certain universal principles of worship are found in its pages. The New Testament doesn't try to prescribe a full list of the essential worship elements that should be present in corporate worship, but it does provide a record of many worship acts and a richly diverse worship vocabulary—both of which contribute to a basic understanding of fundamental elements that should be included in biblical worship.

Jesus himself doesn't teach the details of a new Christian worship practice, but he does articulate for all time the unchanging standard of acceptable worship for all believers—"in spirit and in truth." Overall, the Scriptures don't seem to have as keen an interest in the "packaging" of worship—that is, in its forms and formats—as in its essence and its integrity. So down through the ages of Christian history the church has had the task of translating the biblical materials into "ordered" worship experiences since no such order is provided in the New Testament itself.

> **O**verall, the Scriptures don't seem to have as keen an interest in the "packaging" of worship— that is, in its forms and formats—as in its essence and its integrity.

Isaiah 6:1-11a: A Model for Worship

In many circles today it would be considered hazardous to suggest looking back some 2,750 years to find a viable model for worship in the next century, but that's precisely what I'm doing here. What is it about the worship model presented in Isaiah 6:1-11a that is so strong and effectual that I would urge evangelical congregations to consider revising their current models to conform to this one? There are several reasons:

It is a biblical model. Not only are the elements of this model consistently found in both the Old and New Testaments (thus making them truly "biblical"), but the order of spiritual actions itself derives from the actual, historical encounter with God that Isaiah experienced and recorded in chapter 6 of his prophecy. It's an example of an authentic experience whose elements can be seen again and again throughout the Bible.

It is God-centered. This model keeps God at the center of everything and doesn't allow worship to get off-center. It's clearly God who initiates the experience and who keeps the conversation moving towards its divinely conceived ends.

It is revelation-rich and gives prime place to the Word of God. The customary aspects of divine revelation encountered throughout the Bible are present in this model. God's Word is the major source of God's revelation to us, and this model reflects and embodies that reality.

It is comprehensive in its complement of responses to God. The full gamut of typical worship responses to God is present in this model— from adoration and praise to supplication and intercession. No major omissions are found.

It is dialogical. The relational and conversational nature of true worship is clearly and effectively expressed in this model.

It effectively incorporates the Table with the Word. In services where Communion occurs, the Isaiah 6 model easily accommodates the Lord's Supper service as an integrated component.

It provides a stable, objective approach to worship. There's a downside to being evangelical and free. So much freedom in the content and order of worship can lead to omissions that impoverish and imbalances that distort. In many an evangelical church the elements of public worship are "up for grabs" every time a new pastor appears on the scene. This roller coaster of subjectivity can keep a congregation from understanding the fundamental elements of worship for what they are—abiding absolutes.

It ensures that the congregation isn't consigned to being mere observers or spectators. The "program" model that is so frequently found in evangelical churches today basically assigns to the congregation the role of spectators or observers. The Isaiah 6 model doesn't permit that to happen, for it places the people in the position of continual respondents to the words and actions of God. Inasmuch as worship is what the people do—not what they watch the leaders do—this model helps to improve an inadequate worship practice.

It isn't bound by style, culture, or time. The wonderful applicability and flexibility of this model for different worship styles, cultural expressions, and eras is one of its most commendable values. Whatever packaging the next millennium will wrap worship in, the Isaiah 6 model provides a strong and transferable foundation for that worship.

It provides abundant opportunity for variety and creativity in worship planning. Because Isaiah 6 isn't a fixed liturgy and has no prescribed texts, forms, or even orders of forms, it must be "fleshed out" every week. This keeps worship fresh and vital as we seek the leadership of the Holy Spirit on a continual basis.

Employing this model for forty years has only strengthened and deepened my convictions about its viability and value to the church. There are clearly many ways to do worship. This is a biblical one that may provide your church a pathway to vital worship in the twenty-first century.

In the year that King Uzziah died, I saw the Lord seated on a throne, high and exalted, and the train of his robe filled the temple. Above him were seraphs, each with six wings: With two wings they covered their faces, with two they covered their feet, and with two they were flying. And they were calling to one another: "Holy, holy, holy is the Lord Almighty; the whole earth is full of his glory." At the sound of their voices the doorposts and thresholds shook and the temple was filled with smoke.

"Woe to me!" I cried. "I am ruined! For I am a man of unclean lips, and I live among a people of unclean lips, and my eyes have seen the King, the Lord Almighty."

Then one of the seraphs flew to me with a live coal in his hand, which he had taken with tongs from the altar. With it he touched my mouth and said, "See, this has touched your lips; your guilt is taken away and your sin atoned for."

Then I heard the voice of the Lord saying, "Whom shall I send? And who will go for us?"

And I said, "Here am I. Send me!"

He said, "Go, and tell this people: " 'Be ever hearing, but never understanding; be ever seeing, but never perceiving.' Make the heart of this people calloused; make their ears dull and close their eyes. Otherwise they might see with their eyes, hear with their ears, understand with their hearts, and turn and be healed."

Then I said, "For how long, O Lord?" And he answered: "Until the cities lie ruined and without inhabitant."

—Isaiah 6:1-11a

A Dialogue With God

The worship of God is a dialogue—this is one of the profoundly important truths about biblical worship. This reality distinguishes biblical worship from the false worship of the world's false religions (Psalm 115). The dynamic that propels the worship "conversation" is the rhythmic alternation of revelation and response.

The Isaiah 6 model provides a full and clearly expressed dialogue with God that contains the most comprehensive set of worship responses found in any single worship event recorded in the Bible. As we examine this model, we'll explore:

• God's initiative in divine revelation that prompts us to respond to him in worship,

• five aspects of divine revelation,

• four worship responses prompted by God's self-disclosure, and

• the nine steps of the dialogue (including the New Testament addition of the Communion Table).

Divine Revelation

The term "divine revelation" simply means "God's revealing of himself to us." This is a process—not an event. God's self-disclosure continues throughout our lifetime as he seeks to draw us into ever-deepening understanding and increasingly intimate knowledge of him. In the Isaiah 6 model, every word and every action of God is revelatory. God reveals something of himself in all that he says and does.

Four wonderful and reassuring truths form the basis of God's self-revelation to his people. First, God is knowable. Count it all joy! God can be known—by us. Second, God *wants* us to know him; this

> **G**od is constantly in the process of making himself known to people—especially to those who hunger and thirst after him.

is his heart's desire. Third, God *delights* to be known. Fourth, God is constantly in the process of making himself known to people—especially to those who hunger and thirst after him. These are four plain truth, "good news" assumptions that every sincere worshipper may rejoice in and act upon when engaging with God in worship.

Now what is it that God desires to reveal to us? In the Isaiah 6 text there are five aspects of divine revelation we can observe. Let's examine each one in turn.

The revelation of God's presence. This is a logical prerequisite to any conversation with God. Each party to the conversation must know the other as "present" or no authentic dialogue can take place. Without a word God made his presence known to Isaiah, and in that moment Isaiah saw the Lord, high and lifted up. This kind of divine initiative prompts all true worship. Seeing God with the eyes of faith compels us to worship him. It's his presence, not ours, that makes the greatest impact in worship. His revealing, purifying, guiding, transforming, empowering presence is what sets true worship apart from all other human experiences. Biblical worship is a response to the revelation of God's presence.

> **T**o worship God "in truth" is to worship God not as we think him to be, not as we hope him to be, not as we'd like him to be, but as he is.

The revelation of God's person. It isn't God's intention merely to disclose his presence, but to reveal the glories of his person. God wants us to know him as he is, for God is only worshipped acceptably as he is—not as he is not! To worship God "in truth" is to worship God not as we think him to be, not as we hope him to be, not as we'd like him to be, but as he is.

When people "see God" as he is, worship happens. Matthew 28:17 says, "When they saw him, they worshipped him." The revelation of God's person prompts worship.

The revelation of God's power. The God of the Bible is the omnipotent God—the God of all power. It's his delight to display his powerful deeds before his people and to empower his people to do great deeds in his strength. To behold the great works and the mighty deeds of God moves us to respond to him in awe and wonder and in thanks and praise. Biblical worship is a response to the revelation of God's power.

The revelation of God's purposes. The God of the Bible is a God of purpose. Everything God has ever done has fallen within the scope of his eternal purposes. Everything God has ever said has been consistent with his eternal purposes. God is committed to the ongoing disclosure of his purposes to his people. God wants us to understand his divine intentions. Every Christian's life has been touched by the purposes of God. To be sure, we know in part and understand in part, but God continues to make his purposes more fully known to us so that our lives may be ordered and shaped by him. Our hearts are turned to worship at the revelation of God's eternal purposes.

The revelation of God's plans. The purposes of God ultimately translate into specific plans for our lives. As with Isaiah, so it is with us—God has a wonderful plan for our lives! The God we worship is committed to helping us know and live out his plans for us—"plans to prosper you and not to harm you, plans to give you hope and a future" (Jeremiah 29:11). Such divine revelation prompts us to worship him.

What all this means is that when we come before God to commune with him in the holy dialogue of worship, there are five things we can count on:

- God wants to make his presence known to us;

- God wants to reveal himself, his person, to us;

• God wants to reveal something of his power to us, within us, or among us;

• God wants to make something of his eternal purposes known to us; and

• God wants to reveal something of his plans for our lives.

This is God's "divine disposition" toward us in worship. However, it doesn't mean that we can expect any of these aspects to happen automatically or that we can manipulate God to "perform" for us in any way. We come *in faith* to this conversation, realizing we're totally dependent on God for any revelation whatsoever, and knowing that God in his infinite wisdom and compassion knows what we need most on any given occasion. The God who makes himself known exercises the initiative. Our actions are all responses.

Our Responses to God

Now let's shift our attention to the other side of the worship conversation—our responses to God as worshippers. Isaiah 6 illustrates four fundamental responses to God's revelation.

Adoration and Praise. Since God is the "alpha-point" in worship, it's right and best to focus initially on God and his greatness, not on ourselves and our weakness, our needs, or our unworthiness. The song of the seraphs found in Isaiah 6:3 and Revelation 4:8 provides an excellent model for the way God should be adored when he is worshipped.

Holy, holy, holy is the Lord (God) Almighty;
(who was, and is, and is to come;)
the whole earth is full of his glory.
Isaiah 6:3 (Revelation 4:8)

Continually and without ceasing the seraphs adore the Lord,

singing in antiphonal song the words of this brief, yet profound, act of adoration.[1]

Biblical worship is rich with adoration and praise. Praise is an ongoing celebration of the God in whom we take greatest delight. To love, to adore, to enjoy, to honor, to exalt, to magnify, to glorify, to praise the Lord is our first order of business as the worshippers of God.

> To love, to adore, to enjoy, to honor, to exalt, to magnify, to glorify, to praise the Lord is our first order of business as the worshippers of God.

Contrition and Confession. The revelation of God's holiness to Isaiah had a profound impact on the prophet. Not only did Isaiah see the Lord in this dramatic encounter with God on the throne—he also saw himself, perhaps in a way he had never before experienced. Isaiah is moved to confess his unholiness before a holy God. This act of honesty, contrition, and humility is a moment of truth for the prophet. He immediately understands that, having seen the Lord, the Holy God, he now stands condemned to death.[2] Isaiah understands that his sin separates him from God and bars him from any form of usefulness to God's purposes or plans. Merely seeing God as he is—absolutely holy—the prophet sees himself as he is—a sinful member of a sinful race. And Isaiah does what any one of us would do upon seeing God in this way—he admits his sinfulness to God.

This is a point evangelicals should consider carefully. In much of the evangelical community today, regular confession of sin has all but disappeared from public worship. How do we account for such unconcern over sin in the lives of believers? Could it be a bad case of self-righteousness or spiritual pride? Might it be blatant disregard or insensitivity or mere presumption?

Whatever the reasons, the net result of a non-confessional lifestyle is the dangerous "stockpiling" of sin in our lives. It goes without saying that sin in the church behaves the same way as sin in the world. It destroys, corrupts, divides, robs, perverts, damages, distorts, blinds, weakens, confuses, ruins, and kills. If sin in the world is an offense to God, how much more, sin in the church! We need to remember that Jesus Christ died not only for the sins of the world, but also for the sins of the church. Likewise, the gospel is not only for the world, but also for the church. Confession and contrition should be key elements in worship for all Christians inasmuch as we continue to sin and fall short of the glory of God.

The positive effects of confession are many. For example, in Psalm 51 we can see that confession results in: a clean heart; restored joy; a renewed, steadfast spirit; the gift of forgiveness; restored fellowship with God; the abiding presence of the Holy Spirit; acceptable worship; new zeal for service; fruitfulness in ministry; and the return of the song of praise.

Jesus speaks to this issue in Matthew 5:8: "Blessed are the pure in heart, for they will see God." Sin becomes an obstacle between us and God. If unaddressed, our sin will become a wall that prevents fellowship. It's because *God* loves us and *we* love God that we don't want such a thing to happen. We don't want anything to rob us of the joy of constant fellowship with the One who is dearer than life to us. So we live a life of daily confession. This is the normal Christian life, and our public worship must lead us in this direction.

Submission and Dedication. Our third response in genuine worship should be glad surrender to God. "Here am I. Send me!" (Isaiah 6:8). The act of yielding to the will and purposes of God and committing ourselves to whatever God is revealing at the time is a crucial moment in any worship encounter.

As with everything else in worship, our act of surrender to God is a response to the Word of God—a word of revelation, a word of authority, a word seeking a response. This word may concern our being or our doing. It may relate to our knowing or our serving. It may touch upon our life with God or our relationships with people. In any case, our expected response is to submit ourselves to God, yielding all that we are and have so that his word is obeyed, enacted, and fulfilled in and through our lives.

Two New Testament texts help us understand this response of dedication and commitment. First, consider the words of James:

Humbly accept the word planted in you, which can save you. Do not merely listen to the word, and so deceive yourselves. Do what it says. Anyone who listens to the word but does not do what it says is like a man who looks at his face in a mirror and, after looking at himself, goes away and immediately forgets what he looks like. But the man who looks intently into the perfect law that gives freedom, and continues to do this, not forgetting what he has heard, but doing it—he will be blessed in what he does (James 1:21b-25).

In evangelical worship, we may *enjoy* hearing the Word of God proclaimed, but if that is the extent of our response, we haven't heard it for ourselves or taken it seriously.

This is what Paul declares in Romans 12:1: "Therefore, I urge you, brothers, in view of God's mercy, to offer your bodies as living sacrifices, holy and pleasing to God—this is your spiritual worship." The nature of our response to God is invested in the fascinating pair of words "living sacrifices." On the surface, this seems to be a contradiction in terms inasmuch as "sacrifice" has to do with dying. So what does Paul mean by "living sacrifices"? He is telling us that worship is a *continual* offering up of ourselves to God, not a once-in-a-lifetime experience. Commitment is a day-by-day, hour-by-hour, moment-by-moment yielding up of our entire person to God. This kind of continual submission is a key part of any spiritual act of worship to God.

Supplication and Petition. How encouraging it is for all believers to know that within the framework of authentic worship there is a place where we may lay our burdens before the Lord, make specific requests of him, and intercede for others. In fact, Christians aren't merely permitted to offer requests, but encouraged, even commanded, to do so.

For example, Paul instructs the Ephesian believers to "pray in the Spirit on all occasions with all kinds of prayers and requests. With this in mind, be alert and always keep on praying for all the saints" (Ephesians 6:18). To the Philippians, the apostle writes: "Do not be anxious about anything, but in everything, by prayer and petition, with thanksgiving, present your requests to God" (Philippians 4:6). And in his instructions on worship, Paul writes to Timothy: "I urge, then, first of all, that requests, prayers, intercession and thanksgiving be made for everyone—for kings and all those in authority, that we may live peaceful and quiet lives in all godliness and holiness. This is good, and pleases God our Savior" (I Timothy 2:1-3).

When we lay our requests before God, we acknowledge our total dependence on him for all things. We affirm that God is our source and our sustainer. We honor God by believing he can and will answer our prayers and make a difference in our world.

The four responses in this model span the entire biblical spectrum of prayer.[3] When we add the New Testament institution of Communion to this sequence, the model takes on a completeness that conforms to biblical worship and to the historic practice of the Christian church.

From Biblical Model to Twenty-First Century Reality

Now that we have a biblical model for genuine worship, we need to explore how we can translate this model into an actual service of corporate worship. For convenience, I've divided our model into five scenes, each of which focuses on a different aspect of worship, and explores how we can apply that aspect to evangelical worship in modern times (see "Worship" on page 113).

Scene 1: Revelation and Adoration. Revelation represents a divine process that God alone controls. We can't make God reveal himself or manipulate divine self-disclosure. What, then, can a worship leader do? Actually the worship leader can do only one thing on God's behalf—make provision for the Lord to disclose himself through the primary means of revelation God has used through the centuries, namely, his Word. While not the *exclusive* means of revelation, the Word of God is the *primary* source of revelation that God has chosen to use through the ages. Therefore, every expression of God's revelation should be centered in Scripture, scriptural paraphrases, or other similar expressions of biblical truth from and about God. This opening revelatory segment should focus on affirming and communicating God's presence as well as aspects of God's person and God's purposes. Remember, worship is about God—not about us. Our worship should begin by focusing exclusively on God—his greatness, his glory, his splendor, his majesty.

What types of worship forms can we use for such a special purpose? Instrumental music, Scripture readings, choral music, revelatory songs or hymns such as "Immortal, Invisible, God Only Wise," and multimedia forms that combine Scripture, music, and visual content. In all cases, the lyrics or texts should focus on some aspect of God or his ways. And the music should resonate with our primary concern that God make himself known among his people.

Just as we can't force God to reveal himself, neither can a worship leader make people adore or praise God. All that we can do is make provision for those "who have seen the Lord" in some authentic way to be able to respond to that revelation. Under the guidance of the Holy Spirit, the worship leader should select texts and forms of response that allow worshippers to respond to God in adoration.

The vocabulary of worship in this adoration segment should contain words such as praise, thank, love, exalt, extol, exult, rejoice, magnify, glorify, bless, lift up, shout, fear, long, desire, delight, hunger, thirst, adore, and revere. The actual forms of worship might include hymns, worship songs and choruses, choral anthems, prayers of adoration and praise, psalms or other scriptural acts of praise, instrumental music, other vocal music, and multimedia or audiovisual presentations, which facilitate praise and adoration to God.

Scene 2: Confession and Expiation. When God reveals himself, we are exposed before him. We see ourselves as sinners in need of cleansing and forgiveness. The heart that breaks and repents over sin is the heart God will not despise. The vocabulary of contrition, brokenness, sorrow, humility, shame, grief, repentance, honesty, and admission of guilt is accompanied by pleas for the mercy, the unfailing love, and the great compassion of God. Honest, heart-felt cries for the blotting out of transgressions, the washing away of all iniquity, the cleansing from sin, and the gift of forgiveness result in a pure heart, recovered joy, and a restored relationship.

Forms that can express such spiritual actions include biblical calls to confession, Scripture readings (such as Psalm 51), hymns and other songs of confession, congregational prayer in unison, silent prayer, guided prayer, pastoral prayers of confession, choral music, instrumental music, and other vocal music. Once again in all cases the texts of such acts must be carefully chosen to prompt and facilitate the honest confession of sin. Of course, the worship leader can't make any worshipper confess sin to God, but the leader can and should provide the time and the "raw materials" that allow those who are repentant to express their hearts to God.

God's action in response to sincere, honest confession is the forgiving of our sin and the cleansing of our hearts. The title "Expiation" has been used to describe this revelation of God's character and power. The word "expiation" refers to the covering over of our sin "till not a trace remains," as the hymn writer put it. [4] This special word for forgiveness describes the action of God that in faith is declared to God's people as good news.

The heart of this section lies in a declaration of forgiveness drawn from Scripture, assuring believers that when we confess our sins, God forgives our sins (1 John 1:9). This declaration in Christian tradition has generally taken the form of a pastoral pronouncement. Additional words affirming this truth may be sung in hymns or songs that directly and clearly communicate the reality of forgiveness in the present. Following this action with the giving of thanks for the gift of forgiveness is most fitting.

Scene 3: Proclamation and Dedication. While the focus here is mainly on the revelation of the person, purposes, and plans of God, any of the five dimensions of divine revelation might be encountered during this time. The two primary ways this aspect of worship is customarily expressed are through the reading of a biblical text and a sermon that helps worshippers understand and apply the Word to their lives. In addition, this segment may include a preparatory hymn, chorus, or choral anthem that relates to the content of the sermon text; or a prayer offered before the sermon begins.

Acts of dedication follow as a direct response to God's proclaimed Word. Language such as yield, submit, offer, give, commit, surrender, sacrifice, dedicate, follow, obey, and present can be found in our response. Our acts of submission to God may take the form of hymns or other songs of commitment and dedication, public affirmations of faith, silent reflection and prayer, corporate prayers of commitment, or giving an offering to the Lord.

Scene 4: Communion. When the Lord's Supper is observed, it fits best in the Isaiah 6 framework at this point. Communion has its own fixed contents and actions, which are described in detail in Matthew 26; Mark 14; Luke 22; John 13; and I Corinthians 11. Throughout church history the general shape of this simple rite has remained largely the same. In evangelical churches today, typically a leader will repeat the words and actions of Jesus, and the congregation will participate in response as did the first disciples.

These days it's not typical in most evangelical churches for Communion to be incorporated into every worship service. However, it's worth noting that by the beginning of the second century the rite of the Table was a customary part of all Christian worship services. Since earliest times Christian worship has gathered around the two focal points of the Word and the Table.

Traditionally most of evangelicalism has been Word-centered in its worship; however, the current winds of worship renewal have been bringing about the more frequent observance of Communion and a richer understanding of the role it plays in worship. In 1 Corinthians 11:26a, Paul wrote: "For as often as you eat this bread and drink the cup" (Revised Standard Version). Because neither Jesus nor Paul was specific in informing us as to how often "often" is, we have seen within the various Christian fellowships a great variety of practices, running the gamut from once a year to daily observance. I would not be so bold as to put a numerical value on "often"; however, considering how frequently the early church came to the Table and the rich meaning they attached to it, it seems appropriate to me that evangelical churches should consider making the Table available to their people somewhere in their weekly schedule of services.

Scene 5: Supplication and Commission. Our final scene in this encounter with God contains the act of congregational supplication and the concluding act of sending the congregation back into the world. Supplication consists of the prayers of the people, which may be offered for a variety of needs and in a variety of forms. For example, we might pray for God's intervention as our hearts break over the lostness, the divisions, the injustice, the disease, the pain, and the sadness that plagues our world. These prayers might take the form of unison or guided prayer, silent prayer, the Lord's Prayer, appropriate hymns or worship songs, or a representative pastoral prayer.

After prayers of supplication, the service concludes with a divine charge to the congregation to live out the truth they have heard from God. This is an act of commissioning and sending. As God's people, we are to be salt and light in the world. This commissioning time reminds us of our submission to God and our duty to obey his commands in everyday life.

The acts in this section are generally few: a direct charge to the people, a benediction, and a postlude. However, a congregational affirmation or reiteration of the charge may be spoken or sung.

As scene 5 concludes, the gathered congregation is now scattered to bring the blessings and joy of the "holy place" out into the marketplace. In the people's encounter with God, their minds have been enlightened, their hearts cleansed, their wills realigned, their energies replenished, their vision refocused, their commitment renewed, their mission redefined, their courage restored, their faith deepened, and their passion rekindled.

If they have met the Lord God Almighty, in truth, they can't help but leave changed.

I believe a major aspect of worship renewal in the twenty-first century will focus on the recovery of biblical norms in worship, the restoration of biblical elements to worship, and the realignment of worship with biblical models and paradigms. Building our worship on the Isaiah 6 model allows us to reconnect with all of these trans- forming truths—truths upon which all true worship is founded.

NOTES

1. The psalms are helpful to our understanding of this kind of worship. Adoration is to "Delight yourself in the Lord" (37:4). Enjoying God in the richest, deepest way is what happens in adoration. "To gaze upon the beauty of the Lord" (27:4) describes the singu- lar focus of the adoring mind and heart. "As the deer pants for streams of water, so my soul pants for you, O God. My soul thirsts for God" (42:1, 2). Here the psalmist describes the deep desire after God that springs forth into loving adoration.

2. The word translated "I am ruined!" in the New International Version would be better rendered "I am condemned to die" or, as in the New Living Translation, "My de- struction is sealed."

3. In the simplest typology of biblical prayer we find four basic types: (1) prayers of adoration, praise, and thanksgiving; (2) prayers of contrition, repentance, and confession; (3) prayers of submission, dedication, and commitment; and (4) prayers of petition, suppli- cation, and intercession. All the praying in the Bible is encompassed within this spectrum.

4. Horatius Bonar, "I Lay My Sins on Jesus," (Public Domain).

WORSHIP

A biblical model for evangelical churches drawn
from Isaiah 6:1-11 and the New Testament (with Communion)

ACTS OF GOD		ACTS OF THE PEOPLE
	SCENE 1 Isaiah 6:1-4	
Revelation		
		Adoration
	SCENE 2 Isaiah 6:5-7	
		Confession
Expiation		
	SCENE 3 Isaiah 6:8	
Proclamation		
		Dedication
	SCENE 4 The Gospels 1 Corinthians 11 Communion (when observed)	
	SCENE 5 Isaiah 6:9-11a	
		Supplication
Commission		

Chapter 6

African-American Worship:

Creating a New Worship for the Twenty-First Century

by RICHARD ALLEN FARMER

A s a child growing up in New York City, a product of a strong African-American Baptist church, I lived for Sunday mornings. I could hardly contain myself on a Saturday night. With few exceptions, Sunday was the best day of my week.

Now that those days are in the ever-more-distant past, I have tried to find out why this was so. What was happening on Sundays that shaped the rest of the week? Could it have been the respite from the tedium of school? Could it have been the unique "feel" of Sunday, that "most different" day of the week? Could it have been anticipation of the weekly visit to Grandma and Pop's house in Manhattan? Perhaps.

But I am now sure that what I most looked forward to was the people. A kissing, hugging crew they were—and still are. We children were embraced and encouraged, and we brought great joy and pride to our elders. I looked forward to seeing the folks who gathered at the Trinity Baptist Church in the Bronx.

But there were other realities that drew me. They were more mystical, less tangible. I could not put my finger on it then, but there was mystery in the air. I was overwhelmed by the way the saints in worship seemed delighted to be in that place set aside for worship. There was little clock-watching. There was scarce talk of needing to "get out on time." There was no subsequent appointment that beckoned us. We were there to meet Papa and to sing praises to his name through song, sermon, and varied acts of worship. The late Vance Havner, that wiry Southern evangelist, once said, "It is high time we stopped having worship services that begin at 11 o'clock sharp and end at 12 o'clock dull."

More than forty years have passed since I felt those first waves of excitement, and I am happy to report that I still live for Sundays. I still love the rhythm of a week that begins with a day set aside for contemplation, rumination, proclamation, affirmation, education, variation, provocation, edification, fortification, explanation, adoration, exaltation, magnification, recapitulation, maturation, nullification, ovation, purification, penetration, confrontation, saturation, salvation, transformation, dissemination, preparation, illumination, illustration, rejuvenation, reparation, summation, stabilization, and unification. Though now in possession of an expansive vocabulary, I still cannot describe all that went on on Sundays. I didn't want Sundays to end.

> *The average black church, if it does not have two morning worship celebrations and hence a logistics problem, takes its time in worship. The preacher is not given sixty minutes. He or she is simply given a mandate to help the people experience God.*

African-American Worship

The average black church, if it does not have two morning worship celebrations and hence a logistics problem, takes its time in worship. The preacher is not given sixty minutes. He or she is simply given a mandate to help the people experience God. As long as the folks don't feel time is being wasted, they will stay. I was quite surprised when I went to a predominantly Anglo college and got introduced to the worship style of my other-hued sisters and brothers. There I heard of services that lasted seventy-five minutes, with the preacher apologizing for going past the allotted time. There may be a historical reason for this. In slavery, Sunday was often the only day blacks were permitted to assemble. Even then, that gathering was under the watchful eye of a slave-master or his representative. Sunday afternoon was free for the slaves and worship often ran into the afternoon.

After emancipation, it was still the highest joy of most freed persons to go to church on Sunday and stay all day. As we cruise into the future, I don't foresee a change in this. In fact as racially diverse congregations explore merging, time is one of the factors that will break the negotiations. Different cultures perceive time differently. In Africa, for instance, people are not enslaved to clocks and calendars. An event begins when folks get there and it ends when they are finished doing what they came to do. When I took my thoroughly westernized self to West Africa for the first time in 1994, I had to lay aside my clock watching and simply enjoy the events. In a way, I was getting in touch with my roots. Back on U.S. soil, I found myself wanting the same "we can stay all day" feeling of my childhood Sundays.

The pastor of the church has much to do with how time is perceived by the congregation. If he or she portrays worship as something to be endured or tolerated or gotten through, the congregation picks that up. If, on the other hand, the pastor or leader seems to revel in the thought of time spent before the throne of the Eternal, the people pick that up as well.

In days gone by, the pastor was often the best-educated person in the congregation. He might have been exposed to some reading lessons. He would surely have notable oratorical skill. He came to church prepared to "perform" and he was going to take his time doing so. By the way he conducted himself, the people believed this was important to the preacher. Consequently, it should be important to the saints. Part of the ethos, the nature or disposition of the black church, is that time is much more leisurely spent in worship and celebration.

If you were a college graduate in the black community in the first half of the twentieth century, there were only a few noble professions for you. If you were male you became an insurance executive, a teacher, a politician, a government employee, or a preacher. I am somewhat facetious here, but not much. The calling to the preaching ministry conferred upon any man (and, later, women) instant status.

In most black churches, the pastor is a revered figure. He or she is never addressed by first name, always deferred to in meetings, and granted carte blanche in decisions of the congregation. Each year the congregation celebrates the time of year when that pastor arrived to become the shepherd of the flock. A pastor's anniversary service usually concludes with a large financial gift being given. This is in addition to a salary and other benefits given throughout the year. These days, as the persons in the pews are prospering, it is even easier to "be a financial blessing to our leader." Who is this leader? Why should she or he be held in such high esteem?"

In the black church, the pastor is not merely employed. The congregation, for the most part, believes that this is God's person for this place, this people, this time. To regularly go against that pastor, in some parishioners' thinking, is to go against God himself. Conversely, to be for the pastor is to be for God. This has robbed some folks of the joy and task of thinking through the issues related to life and ministry. They simply sign themselves over to their pastors.

While I use the word "pastor," the word "preacher" is more accurate, for one cannot pastor in the black church unless one can also preach. Preaching is absolutely primary. It is to be a pastor's most prominent gift. There is virtually no model in our churches of a person serving as an executive pastor who does not also preach with both power and authority.

In their excellent, groundbreaking book, *The Black Church in the African American Experience,* Lincoln and Mamiya begin one chapter with, "The sermon, or more accurately, the *preaching* is the focal point of worship in the Black church, and all other activities find their place in some subsidiary relationship."[1] Even if a pastor is a superb counselor, a competent administrator, an outstanding community advocate and a notary public, his or her credibility is measured by the ability to deliver the word of (from) the Lord, to lead the people of the Lord to the throne of the Most High.

Coupled with that verbal proclamation is the prominence of music in the black church. In the 1970s I was introduced to a new model of worship: the Anglo-evangelical tradition. Two musical observations stand out in my memory to this day. I was serving as the musical director of a college touring group. I suggested a song that was quite rhythmic and upbeat. The group enjoyed the song, and one of the singers enthusiastically said it was a great "song for Sunday nights." I quizzically looked at her and asked her what she meant. I then learned that the Anglo church had Sunday morning music and Sunday night music. Such a concept was new to me. At first I thought it was a joke. I then learned that in the Anglo church, conservative music was offered in the morning. In the evening, parishioners return to worship. The atmosphere is more casual, with men leaving their ties home and women wearing pantsuits. The music would be upbeat in the evening.

I never could put this practice to rest, theologically. If a specific song was honoring to God after six in the evening, would he be offended by the song if we sang it seven hours earlier? Was there something about the evening that made some music more acceptable? No one has ever given me a satisfactory answer to this question.

The other observation I made in the '70s was that music was not high on the agenda in Anglo-evangelical worship. The choir often sang one song apart from the congregational songs. This was the so-called special music. Their counterparts in the African-American traditions often gave a mini-concert during worship, singing a minimum of two songs and often three or four. Music is part of the soul of the black church. Other than the preacher, there is no more valued person in the black church than the musician. Commanding top dollar and enjoying significant prestige, the musician is an almost indispensable asset.

Not only are the choirs a very important part of the mix, but the congregation as "singer" is an interesting phenomenon. In the black church tradition, the entire church sings. Often the congregation learns the choirs' songs and can sing them right along with the choral ensembles.

> *Both the sermon and the songs are performed in a context that shapes the proclamation.*

Both the sermon and the songs are performed in a context that shapes the proclamation. In some traditions, the sermons could be picked up, unaltered, and transported to another place without the nature of that proclamation changing. But in the black church, all is done in a certain context. This is especially true for the preaching. Rather than the line-by-line exposition that I became familiar with in the 1970s (which often featured lifeless definitions of Greek words and obscure, irrelevant historical notes), the preaching in the black church was and is heavily weighted toward context.

Churches in poor neighborhoods preach to and about the poor. Preachers with a heavy population of professionals in their audience, aim their remarks to that audience. Freely, many of our best preachers take their political comments, their local concerns, and the passions of their people and weave them into a sermon in such a way that is not intrusive.

In May 1998 I had the privilege of hearing one of the finest preachers in the United States, Dr. Gardner C. Taylor. He is nicknamed "the dean of black preachers" and is pastor emeritus of the Concord Baptist Church of Christ in Brooklyn, New York. At a conference on preaching in Dallas in 1998, Dr. Taylor was preaching on the story of the dry bones in the valley, from Ezekiel 37. He said that the prophet was led back and forth among the bones and saw a great many bones on the floor of the valley. He then went on to say that the preacher's task is to see. We are to see all that is around us and, as Dr. Taylor suggested, to address it. Rather than advocate a separation of the "biblical gospel" from the "social gospel," black preachers tend to look at valleys and comment on them. All this is done while being faithful to the text and the task.

All of these observations regarding the concept of time, the perception of the pastor, the prominence of music, and the primacy of preaching have their delights and their dangers. While I rejoice that the black church takes its time in worship, such a posture could lead to padded hours in which little happens. While we do not wish to be rushed in our adoration of the eternal God, we also do not wish to have our time frittered away by those who have planned little for our edification. Like money, time may be saved as well as spent. A two- to three-hour worship service is not mandatory. An inappropriately relaxed attitude regarding time could lead to slothfulness and a state of unreadiness when opportunities present themselves.

Even the performance of a piece of music is a time issue. In many black gospel songs there is a chorus or refrain which is repeated thirty to forty times in the course of the song. Some would deem this excessive.

Somehow we must find that glorious median wherein we feel not rushed but also not obligated to make an event longer than it need be. In the black church we trust our pastors, who are often the primary worship leaders, to guard our time and make Sunday morning a significant, not-to-be-missed event. I celebrate that.

Likewise, I want to celebrate the way we treat our pastors. While we ought not set up a monarchy or papacy in our Protestant evangelical churches, we ought to highly regard those who lead us, especially those who preach and teach (1 Timothy 5:17-18). Many of our pastors have not had the opportunity to invest in annuity funds, individual retirement accounts, and mutual funds. Their congregations have been their lives and they have spent themselves physically and have often used their personal financial resources to keep those churches afloat. It is fitting and proper that those congregations for whom they have sacrificed treat them well.

As I call for balance in the concept of time, I call for it here. The black church has always treated its leaders well. May that continue without our going to excess and making deities of mere mortals. This treatment of the pastor has much to do with worship, for the pastor is the chief worship leader in our tradition, whether spoken or not. That is, the pastor sets the tone, the mood.

My concern is that while we may honor the pastor, we must be cautious so that our attention to the pastor does not ruin him or her.

As a musician I have enjoyed the prominent place music has in our tradition. As a young artist I could count on getting significant exposure, experience, and playing time in each worship service. We are used throughout the services. In some churches the organist even accompanies the sermon in its concluding minutes. Unfortunately, many a black congregation has been held hostage by an ego-driven musician who thought worship could not go on without him or her. In the name of diversity in worship, we must begin to see music as only one of many vehicles through which our God addresses his people. With the advent of the Willow Creek model in which drama is used frequently, and with the resurgence of liturgical dance and other arts being used in worship, musicians ought to be convinced that they are not indispensable.

With the advent of the Willow Creek model in which drama is used frequently, and with the resurgence of liturgical dance and other arts being used in worship, musicians ought to be convinced that they are not indispensable.

The red flags continue as I analyze the method of preaching which marks many black churches. The proclamation done within a specific context is a delight. However, the danger is that a text may be used merely as a springboard for that preacher's proclamation of a personal agenda. I want to see and hear a sermon that reeks of relevance. I want the preacher to make the text come alive by insightful application. I want my preacher to be a bridge builder, connecting the text with my life. However, I do not and will not appreciate a proclaimer who bends a text to fit her or his own purposes.

Worship in the New Millennium

The next century will present significant challenges to the church in general and the black church in particular. I have heard talk of mergers between Anglo and African-American congregations and of the possible planting of a deliberate multiracial model. It has worked in too few places. One of the reasons it has foundered most of the time is that those diverse congregations cannot agree on length of services. For that matter, they cannot agree on music either. For while on one hand there is simply church music, only the naive would fail to acknowledge that there is Anglo church music and black church music. In the next century, there will be a need for all of us to stretch ourselves and move outside the liturgical box where we are most comfortable.

Music will continue to be prominent. If anything, it will become even more of a gathering tool, bringing people to the church that would not normally be interested. If music continues to be a form of proclamation, we must take care that it not overshadow the verbal proclamation. It is likely that in some churches of the future whose aim will be to reach the lost at any cost, music will be dominant and traditional preaching will be subordinate. This will be a grave error, for what has made the church in the African tradition powerful is its preaching.

In the next century, there will be a need for all of us to stretch ourselves and move outside the liturgical box in which we are most comfortable.

We have yet to sort out the balance between our music and our preaching. There are multitudes of preachers who do not work hard at the craft of preaching or at sermon preparation. Their worship services feature lots of music, with the choirs covering up their leaders' lack of diligence.

As the makeup of our congregations changes, we will have to examine the quality of what we offer in a worship celebration. The persons in the pew will often be as educated as we are, will have traveled as much as we have, will have read as much as we have, and will have high expectations of us. There was a time when leaders could be guaranteed to be several paces ahead of most of their parishioners. However, now the leader of the future church must own up to the fact that their "clientele" is vastly different from that of twenty-five years ago. John Naisbitt and

Patricia Aburdene, in their book *Megatrends 2000,* write, "The 1990s will bring forth a modern renaissance in the visual arts, poetry, dance, theater and music throughout the developed world. It will be in stark contrast with the recent industrial era, where the military was the model and sports was the metaphor."[2] Perhaps knowing this will compel us to broaden our worship presentation so that music is varied and preaching is fresh.

I heard the story of a man in his forties who was very excited to take his two youngsters to the circus. The boys sat unimpressed throughout the entire performance. The father asked the children about their lackluster response, and concluded that children who see a car chase and an explosion several times in the space of one thirty-minute cartoon feature will not be bowled over by a man and a few dancing bears. Our parishioners will have been to the symphony hall, the opera, the outdoor arts festival, and the ballet. We dare not give less quality in worship. If anything, we ought to give them better quality in the church than they observe outside the church, for we know the God who has inspired all that is excellent.

Inasmuch as the African-American church's worship is often used as the paradigm of free, unencumbered worship, I want to make some practical suggestions for those who want to extract the best from that model. I am sure other traditions don't envy the African-American tradition, but they are eager to learn from it and to extract from it valuable components for their own worship. Allow me to offer some suggestions here.

Take Your Time

Again, if you have more than one morning service, you may have time constraints which cannot be challenged. But if you have only one morning worship celebration and only one in the evening, take your time. Diners who are being well fed do not leave the table.

Likewise, worshippers who are deriving meaningful spiritual food from the worship service will not leave simply because sixty minutes have passed. Allow plenteous time for prayer, which is often given two minutes in the average worship celebration. Allow time for information about mission activity to be shared. That is, let the folks know what's happening outside the congregation and outside the country. Let the choir sing. They could even sing more than one song per service! If there are those who must leave, let them leave. The majority of folks will stay, for what happens in us and to us on a given Sunday morning happens nowhere else.

In the future, people will come to worship to stay a while. They will find at the worship center a plethora of needs being met. In a full circle kind of movement, the church will once again become the center of a community's life. The building will house amenities that make it attractive for people to come and, not only hear from God, but build social relationships as well. Take your time. Let it happen.

Charlie Coleman is now with the Lord. For many years, he worked as the custodian of the church I pastored in Pittsburgh, Pennsylvania. Charlie was notorious for turning the lights off in the building if he felt parishioners were lingering too long. While they were enjoying the afterglow of a meeting or worship celebration or choir rehearsal, Charlie would start flicking the lights. That was our signal to move along. In the future, the custodians will stay longer. Suffer it to be so.

See Your Pastor Differently

I am not advocating giving to a pastor dictatorial powers, as is often the case in the black church. However, we will see many capable men and women leave ministry in the twenty-first century if they sense they have no significant power. One of the hallmarks of the black church is the authority and confidence with which our pastors speak. Worship takes on a magnificent power when the leader of worship does not appear to be always asking permission.

Some years ago I was ministering in a New England church on a Sunday morning. While we were in worship it began to snow quite heavily. We had scheduled a Sunday evening service as well. The pastor got up at the conclusion of the morning worship, looked out the window, and said to the congregation: "Well, what do you think we ought to do about this evening? Shall we come back or just stay at home because of the snow?"

I chuckled inside because this pastor didn't have the confidence to simply make a decision. Free your pastor to do what needs to be done—especially in worship. For nearly four hundred years, black folks have struggled with what it means to be free. The church is no place for fetters to be placed on people. If we want to see worship blossom, we must free the very men and women whom we say we trust. Let them do what we need done. Free the priests to bring the people to God.

Let the People Sing

Who came up with the policy, "We shall have one special number per service"? Or, "There shall be a package of special music for six minutes and no more"? Why not unleash the people who bring us music? Why not demand that the congregation sing unto the Lord? Why not feature instruments other than piano, organ, electronic keyboard, and drums? Why not commission composers and arrangers to create a piece for the choirs and congregation?

During the 1950s through the 1980s, congregations had song

Let's not lose the concept of song as a significant component of worship. Let the people sing!

leaders. Now we have worship leaders, which is more accurate terminology. However, let's not lose the concept of song as a significant component of worship. Let the people sing!

Let them sing often. Let them sing strongly. The power of music is outrageously compelling, drawing in the most unsuspecting listener. In the future, the magnetic power of music will be unleashed. People will not flock to places in which they perceive the bards bound. Music is the most accessible vehicle through which parishioners may declare the deeds of God and their faith in him. We cannot all preach together. We can't usher together. Nor can we provide childcare as a large group. *But we can sing in unison.* We can lift our voices together in praise to our magnificent God. In the future, congregations will want more music, not less.

We cannot all preach together. We can't usher together. Nor can we provide childcare as a large group. But we can sing in unison.

In his book in which he analyzes the power of blues and spirituals, James Cone talks about Saturday nights in Bearden, Arkansas: "The men and women gathered around the juke box had worked long hours during the week in saw mills and factories; by Saturday night they were tired and weary. They needed to express their moods and feelings, their joys and sorrows. They needed to refresh their spirits in the sound and rhythm of black humanity. And they did."[3]

I want that said of the church. On Sunday morning, which is prime time, people will gather around the worship event, weary from a week that has been long and difficult. They will need to express their pain, their moods, and their feelings. And they need to do so in the sound and rhythm of the saints.

Finally, let me suggest that in the years to come, one of the gifts of the black church will be its contextual preaching. Nearly every black preacher you will ever hear will preach the story of the Exodus as if she or he is leading the people out of some wilderness. They will preach the story of Jesus stilling the storm in such a way that any figurative storm that a parishioner is dealing with will pale in comparison to the power of Christ. In this preaching style, Zacchaeus did not merely climb a tree. He climbed up and over every obstacle that the person in the pew has encountered. When we preach about demons, we do not merely preach about the powers of Satan as seen in the tempting of the saints. We also speak about the demons in city hall, the governor's mansion, the school system, and the White House. We speak about the dark forces of racism and oppression and hopelessness. Be gone the days in which we simply tell what the text says without telling our folks what it means.

In the next century, people will yawn at the preaching of the Word of God if we fail to put it in a casing that makes sense. Make it live. Make the text jump off the page. You want the excitement in your congregation that you see in the black church? Then borrow that rich tradition of looking behind the lines of the text. Sit where the saints sit. Feel what they feel. Ask the questions they would ask. We go into the next millennium borrowing the best of each tradition and rejoicing that God is not nearly as narrow or as bound as we are.

Ultimately, we will, if we are smart, borrow from a number of sources in order to improve our lot. We will learn from our Latino sisters and brothers. We will borrow from the Asian tradition. We will celebrate the way God uses the Anglo tradition, and we will go confidently into the unknown with this known: God is at work within and among us. Rather than boasting that we are colorblind, we will acknowledge the rainbow around us and learn from each hue. Rather than merely tolerating other cultures, which tends to be our posture,

Rather than boasting that we are colorblind, we will acknowledge the rainbow around us and learn from each hue.

the future will dare us to celebrate diversity.

A look at history will lead us to genuine celebration. Such a look will challenge our arrogance, our feelings of smug superiority. Paul Johnson has said, "The study of history is a powerful antidote to contemporary arrogance. It is humbling to discover how many of our glib assumptions, which seem to us novel and plausible, have been tested before, not once but many times and in innumerable guises; and discovered to be, at great human cost, wholly false."[4]

In the twenty-first century, we fully expect that the church will challenge the false assumptions that it has been saddled with. It will test the spirits of its culture and ignore those it finds going against biblical mandates. It will see the varied cultural expressions of the body of Christ, the church, as contributing entities to its own diversity, rather than as aberrations to be gawked at or endured. The black church will be treasured for its unique contribution to the life of the worshipping body called the church.

After the assassination of Mahatma Gandhi, Prime Minister of India Jawaharlal Nehru, delivered a stirring tribute to the late pacifist, Nehru's lifelong friend. Of Gandhi, Nehru said:

> He was perhaps the greatest symbol of the India of the past, and may I say, of the India of the future, that we could have had. We stand on this perilous edge of the present, between that past and the future to be, and we face all manner of perils. And the greatest peril is sometimes the lack of faith which comes to us, the sense of frustration that comes to us, the sinking of the heart and of the spirit that comes to us when we see ideals go overboard, when we see the great things that we talked about somehow pass into empty words, and life taking a different course. Yet, I do believe that perhaps this period will pass soon enough.[5]

Isn't that a great tribute? Borrowing from Nehru, let me suggest that we, the church, stand on the perilous edge of the present, between our ecclesiastical past and the future to be. Our greatest peril may be our failure to appreciate the wondrous contributions of the people of color to the fabric of the universal body of Christ. We see all of our talk about unity die as empty words and our high ideals destroyed by our narrowness. I still believe that this period will pass. I march confidently into the future. Transformed. Worshipping. Black.

Let the church say "Amen!"

NOTES

1. C Eric Lincoln and Lawrence H. Mamiya, *The Black Church in the African American Experience* (Durham, NC: Duke University Press, 1990), 346.

2. John Naisbitt and Patricia Aburdene, *Megatrends 2000* (New York, NY: Avon Books, 1991), 51.

3. James H. Cone, *The Spirituals and the Blues* (Maryknoll, NY: Orbis Books, 1992), 1.

4. Quote from Thomas Sowell, *Migrations and Cultures: A World View,* (New York, NY: BasicBooks, 1997), 371.

5. Quote from William Safire, ed., *Lend Me Your Ears: Great Speeches in History* (New York, NY: W.W. Norton and Company, 1997), 210.

Chapter 7

Charismatic Worship:

Embracing a Worship Reformation

by JACK W. HAYFORD

T he very foundation of the church was shaken nearly a half-millennium ago when Martin Luther nailed his Theses to the church door in Wittenburg. The thrust that propelled the Reformation forward was a challenge issued to the church to turn and face the reality of God's Word. Unfortunately, the faith of Christians prior to the Reformation was bound and dominated by the religious institutions and traditions of the day. As God's Word confronted these man-made institutions, the people of God were slowly released from them.

T oday we are due for another reformation— a Reformation of Worship.

Today we are due for another reformation—a Reformation of Worship.

It's important to recognize, however, that a Reformation of Worship is already in progress. Those who would suggest that the church is merely going through another phase have failed to recognize the significance of this contemporary worship reformation. The long-standing definition of worship as an hour's exercise on Sunday is being redefined and unwrapped. This doesn't necessarily imply that valued traditions must be discarded. Rather, they must be refilled with meaning relevant to Christians today.

The early Reformation, which was motivated by the courageous leadership of Huss, Luther, Calvin, Zwingli, Knox, and others, resulted in unchaining the faith of God's people. A new faith, not bound by church tradition, began to fill the hearts of millions. Spiritual slavery was cast aside as God's Word began redefining what it meant to be a Christian.

Similarly, a reformation needs to sweep through Christian worship today, providing spiritual food for a relationally disintegrating and spiritually thirsty society. The power of worship needs to be reawakened in the lives of people today, and questions that recur need to be addressed, such as What are we here for? and Why are things the way they are?

Indeed, worship holds the solution to the contemporary dilemma for a drugged, drunken, suicidal-prone, and self-absorbed generation.

A true Reformation of Worship won't occur, however, without pain and confrontation. A reformation of this nature will challenge the tidiness of our worship systems. Just as Luther's voice irritated existing religious structures, a modern worship reformation will "bite" the neatness of prescribed worship ideas and methods. In fact, this "bite" will demand the sacrifice of everything that is derived by humans and seeks to secure itself in human systems, thought, and practice. It will call for casting aside all that

> *Just as Luther's voice irritated existing religious structures, a modern worship reformation will "bite" the neatness of prescribed worship ideas and methods.*

we humans try to preserve for our own interests.

Whenever we try to interact with God's Word with our human desires, there is a "bite." As much as we want beauty and comfort, we must understand that these factors are secondary to God. God resists everything that obstructs us from entering into a deep, worshipful relationship with him. This includes worship that is bound by man-made traditions and religious structures.

Tradition

There is no part of the human experience that is more shaped by tradition than our worship. We love tradition and hate it at the same time. It poses a significant dilemma for us: We might die to preserve it, but if the truth were known, we can't live with it. Why? Because the force of our worship tradition often overrides the truth of God's Word. Although we usually won't acknowledge it, we prefer worship styles that suit our own comfort, personal taste, and traditions to the "bite" that comes when we try to weave God's Word with our own motives.

The modern worship reformation is here and is challenging us to discard our security blanket of "warm fuzzy" feelings about worship. It's pressing against the resistance of human pride and the preoccupation of comfort.

Worship Defined

Worship won't begin to make sense until we understand its place in God's total plan. God gave worship so that we might become partners in his highest purposes. If we are obedient to God's design for worship, we place ourselves under his kingdom rule. Most importantly, however, obedient worship makes possible a reinvestment of God's rule among humankind. Whatever we have lost through defiled worship patterns, God can restore through obedient worship. It's a biblical principle—God extends incredible strength to those who are loyal to him and worship within his will. "For the eyes of the Lord range throughout the earth to strengthen those whose hearts are fully committed to him" (2 Chronicles 16:9).

> *The question we Christians must face today is whether or not we're willing to face the "bite" of a worship reformation. The consequences of either choice are tremendous.*

The question we Christians must face today is whether or not we're willing to face the "bite" of a worship reformation. The consequences of either choice are tremendous.

For many people, their primary understanding of the purpose for worship is simply to gather and bless God by worshipping him. But there is a second purpose as well: the human need for worship.

True worshippers must worship God in the power of his Spirit and his truth (John 4:24). Therefore, true worship comes to us as a gift from God for his people. This implies that, while God is to be the focus of our praise, we should also find the "gift" of worship to be a blessing for us that leads to significant joy, purpose, and fulfillment. This, however, leads to an interesting question: If one of the purposes of worship is to bring restoration and fulfillment to people, why, in a typical worship service, do we often find ourselves bored rather than blessed? The gift of worship is meant to be a blessing rather than a routine and dreary chore. If worship is based on biblical principles, it becomes much more than a God-built desire to motivate people to stroke a heavenly ego. The Scriptures consistently reveal that worship releases blessings in two directions—both toward God and toward God's people. When this kind of true worship occurs, we allow God the opportunity to release, renew, redeem, and restore us.

The Key to Successful Worship

One of Jesus' most profound statements about worship came as he offered the woman at the well an opportunity to empty her cup of loneliness and brokenness and have it filled with his love (John 4:3-26). This passage illustrates that worship involves an exchange between God and his people. Healing and joy flow into our lives from heaven as we offer ourselves to God as living sacrifices (Romans 12:1).

The key to successful worship is in allowing it to serve as a means to meet human need. Successful worship isn't discovered in a better program, rather it's a natural expression of a congregation that understands God's power and purpose in worship and willingly brings itself into alignment with that purpose.

On the other hand, worship won't be successful in a spiritual sense if any of these four characteristics are present:

• If worship is used as a self-serving tool.

• If the vision or meaning of worship has been corrupted.

• If services are manipulated to serve human needs.

• If God is expected to jump through a series of hoops to meet human desires.

Worship is a human opportunity to invite God's power and presence to move among those gathered to worship him. True worship draws non-Christians to Christ. Hearts that were previously unyielding can sense the power of God's presence in true worship. In a very significant and real sense, worship is a great key to evangelism. Worship provides God an opportunity to respond to the hunger of earnest hearts. Real worship will satisfy the hunger and thirst of men, women, and children.

The Pharisees turned the Sabbath into an impossible system of ritualistic observances that prohibited joyous participation. In the same way, for successful worship to occur, our own modern traditions must be confronted, examined, and, if necessary, adjusted. This is an absolute necessity if God's purpose for worship—to infuse his people with joy, blessing, purpose, and fulfillment—is ever to be restored. Whenever traditional worship becomes a mere formality, chances are it will lose its contact with God. Good preaching isn't enough to bring people completely into God's presence. There must be teamwork between the Spirit and the Word. The Holy Spirit softens the hearts of worshippers as God's Word opens their eyes.

One of the most significant and important points to understand about worship is that it's *the point* of the church's being, not just *a part*. If worship is true to God's purpose and plan, it will serve as the "front line" of Christ's power to change and restore human lives.

Just as the apostle Paul proclaimed that "the message of the cross is foolishness to those who are perishing" (1 Corinthians 1:18), the power of worship doesn't make sense to a world that operates strictly by dollars, numbers of people, and strategic weapons. God, on the other hand, operates on the power of praise, sacrifice, and the humility of the heart.

In reality, our resistance against a modern worship reformation is simply due to our fear—fear that if we transform our worship and place it under God's control, we will lose control. The Pharaohs of our souls must be slain. Why? True worship holds the key to unshackling our future potential. True worship is so powerful that it will change our attitudes toward God and toward each other.

Probably the best way to gain a practical understanding of true worship is to examine a biblical case study.

A Biblical Case Study: David

The life and music of David provide some practical and creative insights into broadening the horizons of worship. During his life, David exhibited qualities of the heart and practices in praise that set him apart. He was very aware that God's desire was to dwell among his people. God desired to bless people with victory, mercy, and loving-kindness. As we observe the worship life of David, it's impossible to avoid one powerful conclusion: *Not only is God unopposed to emotional, expressive worship—he welcomes it.*

David revealed a heart that was filled with passion for God when he wrote: "O God, you are my God, earnestly I seek you; my soul thirsts for you, my body longs for you, in a dry and weary land where there is no water. I have seen you in the sanctuary and beheld your power and your glory" (Psalm 63:1-2).

These words illustrate David's passionate desire for God's presence in his life. Because David highly valued worship, one of his objectives was to bring the ark of God into Jerusalem. David knew the value of God's presence during worship, so he prepared a new place for the ark to dwell: "They brought the ark of God and set it inside the tent that David had pitched for it" (1 Chronicles 16:1a).

The first priority of David upon the arrival of the ark was to conduct a great feast. The feast powerfully illustrated that whenever worship is renewed, people are both fed and filled with joy. The feast that marked the renewal of worship also marked the occasion of David introducing several new worship songs. Thus the feast was filled with music of praise and worship and was "accompanied by musical instruments: lyres, harps and cymbals" (1 Chronicles 15:16).

The story of David bringing the ark into Jerusalem provides several practical lessons about our modern attempts to renew and reform worship. One of the best lessons we can learn comes from an error David made.

Apparently David had either forgotten or was ignorant of the fact that, from the days of Moses, God required that whenever the ark was moved, it had to be carried on the shoulders of the priests (Numbers 4:5-15).

Unfortunately, those instructions were neglected, and Uzzah lost his life as a result of the incident. David was reminded in a tough way that obedience to God is more important than enthusiasm. The method used to transport the ark demonstrated the result of what happens when a human interest is out of synchronization with God's plan. The death of Uzzah provided a tragic end to what seemed like the start of something wonderful.

David's experience provides a practical lesson for us. Before we rush ahead in our zeal for God, we need to be sure what we are doing is in line with God's plan and obedient to his will. As we enthusiastically make new plans for worship, we must consider whether or not we're forging ahead without God. It's not that we aren't sincere. David was quite sincere in bringing people into the real presence of God. But he failed because he didn't take God's commands into account. And the result was death. Our enthusiastic attempts at worship and bringing people into the real presence of God can come to the same end if we fail to accept God's terms.

There are always people who resist sponta-neous, expressive, and joy-filled worship. There is always a Michal.

David was willing to admit he was wrong and start over again. The second time, however, he was careful to fulfill God's Word in the process. His attempt was successful and resulted in rejoicing, sounds of trumpets filling the air, resounding joy, and dancing. Concern for retaining an air of sophistication was cast aside. Unfortunately, there remained one problem that David would have to face before nightfall.

There are always people who resist spontaneous, expressive, and joy-filled worship. There is always a Michal.

A Biblical Case Study: Michal

With all the people watching, David celebrated God's presence by "leaping and dancing before the Lord" (2 Samuel 6:16). David's wife Michal became infuriated at his spectacle, even though his dance honored God. But as Michal watched, "she despised him in her heart." When David arrived at home, she unloaded on him. As a result of her rejection, Michal had to face another kind of music—barrenness (2 Samuel 6:23).

Michal's experience tells a story that's been told a hundred times over, and one that the modern worship reformation demands to be told again. It's a message of warning of what can happen when human tastes and agendas reject the childlike simplicity and spontaneity that pleases God in worship.

Barren, childless, fruitless, and unproductive are all adjectives that not only describe Michal, but also describe worship that's neither pleasing to God nor obedient to his Word.

Michal continued to live her life, but it was a cardboard existence. She existed without all the joys that might have been hers. Congregations who fail to understand the purpose and true meaning of worship and who fail to worship according to God's Word are subject to the same existence.

Michal's syndrome characterizes those of us who are more preoccupied with style, dignity, sophistication, and tradition than with being childlike and expressive in praising God. Expressiveness in

Michal's experience tells a story that's been told a hundred times over, and one that the modern worship reformation demands to be told again. It's a message of warning of what can happen when human tastes and agendas reject the childlike simplicity and spontaneity that pleases God in worship.

worship involves openness, simplicity, spontaneity, active participation, and any other assertive display of praise. Expressiveness in worship, however, consistently invokes strong reactions from God's people—from wild support to angered resistance.

People who reject expressive worship, such as that demonstrated by David, always seem to find some justification for their opinion. For example:

• Some people need a lot of enthusiasm in worship; mature worshippers don't.

• Worship style is a matter of an individual's educational or cultural background. Those who are more educated desire worship that is highly dignified, traditional, and structured.

• Emotionalism causes worshippers to lose objectivity in worship.

• Everyone should worship God in his or her own way and according to individual beliefs.

• God looks at the heart. What we do in worship doesn't add or take away from our relationship with God.

Just as it was for Michal, barrenness is a high price to pay for one's dignity in worship.

The case study of David and Michal provides many insights into biblical worship; however, there are two that stand out as most significant and worth summarizing.

1. We need to examine our worship to see whether it's obedient to God's Word. We would be wise to learn from David's error and not, out of enthusiasm, rush ahead without the assurance that we are being

obedient to God's commands.

2. The rejection of childlike simplicity and joyful expressiveness in worship can quickly lead to spiritual barrenness in a congregation.

Expressiveness in Worship

Any discussion about worship should be centered on biblical facts. One of the most visible characteristics of biblical worship is that of expression that involves the body, the spirit, the heart, the intellect, and the emotions. Worship expressions illustrated in the Bible include

- lively and joyous singing involving all worshippers,

- spontaneous and verbal praises from those present in worship,

- humble kneeling or lying prostrate before the Lord,

- hands upraised and stretched forth in worship, and

- hands clapping in tempo with music and as applause expressed to God.

There are some who see these expressions in the modern church and react with accusations: Disorder! Emotionalism! Charismatic chaos! The most effective method for shortcutting accusations is simply to look into the Word of God.

Again, the story of David provides an important point of reference. Even though David was human and made mistakes, his heart was endorsed by God (1 Samuel 13:14). Because of that endorsement, David provides a solid source of guidance for a study of biblical worship. David's directives in worship provided significant influence for worship traits that developed in the first century and remain valid today.

One of the most important elements in biblical worship is that of *sacrifice*. The human tendency has always been against sacrificing our own ways to God. Whatever resistance a person feels toward

B*efore we can experience a true sense of biblical worship, we must allow God's Word to command our behavior. This includes active participation in expressive worship.*

expressive worship can't be justified in biblical terms. The Word of God mandates that the Bible is the arbitrator of human taste rather than the culture. Before we can experience a true sense of biblical worship, we must allow God's Word to command our behavior. This includes active participation in expressive worship.

There are a variety of references to expressive prayer and worship in the New Testament.

Singing:

"Therefore I will praise you among the Gentiles; I will sing hymns to your name" (Romans 15:9).

"Sing praises to him, all you peoples" (Romans 15:11b).

Praising:

"But you are a chosen people, a royal priesthood, a holy nation, a people belonging to God, that you may declare the praises of him who called you out of darkness into his wonderful light" (1 Peter 2:9).

Upraised hands:

"I want men everywhere to lift up holy hands in prayer" (1 Timothy 2:8a).

Kneeling:

"When he had said this, he knelt down with all of them and prayed" (Acts 20:36).

"I kneel before the Father, from whom his whole family in heaven and on earth derives its name" (Ephesians 3:14-15).

Offerings:

"Now about the collection for God's people: Do what I told the Galatian churches to do. On the first day of every week, each one of you should set aside a sum of money in keeping with his income, saving it up… Then, when I arrive, I will give letters of introduction to the men you approve and send them with your gift to Jerusalem" (1 Corinthians 16:1-3).

Reading the Scriptures:

"Devote yourself to the public reading of Scripture, to preaching and to teaching" (1 Timothy 4:13b).

This combination of elements illustrates that New Testament worship comprises a full array of expression. Biblical worship isn't a one dimension activity. It involves a combination of reason, spiritual intuition, and emotions. Paul illustrates this well by his words: "So what shall I do? I will pray with my spirit, but I will also pray with my mind; I will sing with my spirit, but I will also sing with my mind" (1 Corinthians 14:15). The words of Scripture reveal that worship is neither an exercise of barren intellectualism or thoughtless emotion. Worship involves the total human being: spirit, mind, emotions, and body.

A worshipper clinging to his or her "right" not to participate in expressive worship is directly confronted by God's Word: "Clap your hands, all you nations; shout to God with cries of joy" (Psalm 47:1). Even with biblical directives before us, however, there are those who assert

> *A worshipper clinging to his or her "right" not to participate in expressive worship is directly confronted by God's Word.*

that "people who applaud or make noise or offer verbal praise in worship aren't exercising reverence toward God." It's possible that the worshippers to which they refer really aren't being reverent towards God. That's an issue of the heart—not of expression. In any case, one person's questionable actions in worship do not justify another person's decision to ignore the Bible's commands.

Of course, noise isn't the objective in expressive worship. Too often, however, silence or reserved quietness dominate our worship because we consistently identify silence with reverence. The Scriptures often speak to the contrary. In fact, there are some situations in which the least appropriate response is silence. Psalm 98:4 reminds us to "Shout for joy to the Lord, all the earth, burst into jubilant song with music." Joyful sounds ringing forth in worship may take on many forms—including applause, laughter, praise, and singing. And all of these forms express our reverence for God.

The modern worship reformation challenges us, as do the examples of David, to experience the release of joy in expressive worship.

Whenever expressive worship is merely tolerated and scattered, a congregation won't move beyond being a miscellaneous assortment of worshippers toward a cohesive, worshipful body.

There are worshippers who choose to sit quietly and remain indifferent as expressive worship occurs around them. Whenever expressive worship is merely tolerated and scattered, a congregation won't move beyond being a miscellaneous assortment of worshippers toward a cohesive, worshipful body. Unfortunately, until a congregation becomes a worshipful body, true freedom of expression in worship will remain subdued.

Worshipping at New Levels

From new songs to new instruments to new demonstrations of praise, it was David who first directly challenged God's people to a new depth in worship. David's challenge called for a worship reformation. It was a reformation characterized by newness surrounding everything. David's expressiveness was at the heart of this new worship just as Michal's resistance was at its throat.

David's example of leadership during this time of great change holds promise for those who are leading the path for today's worship reformation. There will be challenges and obstacles; there will be Michals; there will be pain; there will be mistakes; there will be ex-

> *The reward of reformed worship is the enthroned presence of God.*

cuses. But the reward of reformed worship is the enthroned presence of God.

The price is worth the freedom of expression and worship in the presence of God himself.

The Power of Music in Worship

There are eighty-five Scripture passages that exhort God's people to sing praises to the Lord. Most of them are found in the psalms, but several come from the New Testament.

The New Testament specifically offers guidelines for music and singing in worship by issuing the directive to sing psalms, hymns, and spiritual songs: "Let the Word of Christ dwell in you richly as you teach and admonish one another with all wisdom, and as you sing psalms, hymns, and spiritual songs with gratitude in your hearts to God" (Colossians 3:16).

This passage explicitly states that the fruitful implanting of God's Word is linked to singing and worshipping. Most of us think of these two elements as separate. Singing in worship is often thought of as inspirational while the exhortation of God's Word as merely instructional. The words of Scripture, however, challenge us to understand that human intellect and emotion are integrated through singing in worship.

Spiritual singing is necessary for God's Word to be completely assimilated in our hearts and minds. Worship that is spirit-filled provides insurance against simply learning facts from the Bible instead of receiving power through its teaching. With this in mind, Paul's second mention of singing becomes more meaningful: "Do not get drunk on wine, which leads to debauchery. Instead, be filled with the Spirit. Speak to one another with psalms, hymns and spiritual songs. Sing and make music in your heart to the Lord" (Ephesians 5:18-19).

Paul's words hold no mystery. God's Word is clear. If a person desires to walk in God's will, he or she must avoid the world's spirit and instead be filled with God's Spirit. Meaningful singing in worship is the way to do both.

In these two epistles, Paul directs that God's people sing three different types of songs: psalms, hymns, and spiritual songs. An important point to recognize from this passage is that a variety of songs are to be used in worship.

With the importance the Scriptures place on singing and with music so universally enjoyed, it's often difficult to understand why the music of the church is often the focal point of problems and difficulty. Unfortunately, the difficulty often takes the form of polarization.

On one hand, there are those who are so wrapped up in keeping tradition that they won't sing anything that's not printed in the hymnal. Hanging onto tradition in this manner is tragic. Those who do so scorn God's Word by their resistance to employing a variety of musical forms in worship. They exalt a hymnal of human creation, beautiful though it may be, above God's Word.

On the other hand, in some renewal congregations, traditional hymns have been discarded as irrelevant artifacts of a different era. What they fail to realize is that hymns provide music that links us to our predecessors and has stood the test of time.

God's Word reveals the necessity of a variety of music in worship. Biblical worship calls for hymns to be fused into our hearts and souls along with newer spiritual songs and informal choruses.

Introducing new music into worship can be difficult. Fortunately, there are a few proven guidelines to consider when teaching any new form of singing or element of worship:

• Introduce the biblical basis for the addition. People typically respond to the truth when they see it, so it's vital to show them how the new component is grounded in God's Word.

• Don't expect too much too quickly. Rushing something often creates a sense of unrest and can result in failure. Remember that people are likened to sheep in the Bible, not horses.

• Finally, don't propose something new as an opponent of something old. Lead the congregation into a new form of music or worship, introducing it as an addition, rather than a total replacement.

A close examination of the Bible reveals that singing is not only an offering of praise for what God has done in our lives, but an instrument for contributing to an immense spiritual breakthrough. Miracles and powerful works can ride on the wings of a song. Worship that is filled with singing will shake Satan's domain and extend God's kingdom.

The importance of music to the modern Reformation of Worship can't be overstated. Singing will soften hearts and allow the Word of God to convict hardened souls. Worshipful singing will serve as the cutting edge of a Reformation of Worship.

Certainly, committing to a worship reformation only for the sake of change is pointless. But a reformation that ushers God's people into his presence is the path that leads to life. Human-made worship traditions and forms must be confronted so that God's people can be released to express themselves in true biblical worship. David took a chance and, even though Michal protested, the tabernacle was filled with praises to the Lord.

It's time we took a chance again.

(Adopted with permission from the book *Worship His Majesty,* Word Publishing.)

Chapter 8

Gen-X Worship:

A Model for a New Generation

by JOHN S. MILLER

Being born in 1972 affords me a certain number of quirks, difficulties, and freedoms. My generation has a number of labels, some reasonably accurate. Most, however, are rash generalizations: Generation X, Baby Busters, Thirteenth Gen, Slacker Generation, Generation Angst, Lost Generation, Fatherless Generation. For the most part, if you have had any contact with people from this generation, then you've found that the "slacker" connotation is a foolishly cast stereotype. In their book *Inside the Soul of a New Generation,* Tim Celek and Dieter Zander comment:

> Besides jokes about angst, Busters commonly must learn to deal with a frustrating foe: the stereotype of the slacker. In our decade of dealing with Busters, we've found this to be utter nonsense. In 1994 Newsweek devoted a cover story to debunking myths about the Busters. Jeff Giles' "Generalizations X" placed the slacker story as Myth Number One, noting that "most of the bad PR comes from Boomers, who seem engaged in what

Coupland called 'clique maintenance.' "[1]

Before we all engage in the standard blame-displacement discussion, I would rather move on to the more striking qualities inherent in our generation. This generation is perhaps the most loyal, dedicated, community-oriented, motivated, emotional, and determined group of people ever to exist in recent history. There are more people in Generation X involved with volunteer organizations than any other generation ever.

I believe this behavior has been prompted, in part, by relational starvation. Most Gen Xers grew up in either a divorced home, a single-parent home, or an absentee-parent home. Some grew up with practically no home at all. I find it interesting that, for a group of people who have more than enough reason to be anti-relationship, most choose to search passionately for significant, meaningful, and healthy relationships.

Churches and ministries catering to Gen Xers tend to find a highly social- and community-oriented body attending their events. Not only are we searching for relationships with other people, but with the onset of the postmodern paradigm shift, more and more people are open to the idea of a relationship with the supernatural. We have the unique opportunity of introducing people to God as they search for supernatural solutions. All of these elements suggest certain components that should be incorporated into the driving factors of each ministry's and church's core values. Not only should we consider these factors in the visionary and missionary stages, but in programming and event environments as well.

Before anyone begins to speculate as to whether I'm suggesting we compromise the message at all, be assured that I'm addressing method issues and not even remotely proposing that we begin to compromise the message of Christ's life. The message should always remain the same. It needs no adaptation or manipulation. It stands on its own accord—flawless and incredible—even two thousand years after the time of Christ. Instead, our focus should be this: How do we provide an environment where people can enter into vibrant relationships with God and others?

Gen-X Core Values

At The Next Level Church we have developed four core values to help us to provide the type of environment we feel allows all of these things to take place. I begin here because I want you to understand the importance we place on worship and therefore how I have chosen to cast vision in the area of worship. In Colossians 3:12-17, we see the scriptural model for all of our core values:

Therefore, as God's chosen people, holy and dearly loved, clothe yourselves with compassion, kindness, humility, gentleness and patience. Bear with each other and forgive whatever grievances you may have against one another. Forgive as the Lord forgave you. And over all these virtues put on love, which binds them all together in perfect unity.

Let the peace of Christ rule in your hearts, since as members of one body you were called to peace. And be thankful. Let the word of Christ dwell in you richly as you teach and admonish one another with all wisdom, and as you sing psalms, hymns and spiritual songs with gratitude in your hearts to God. And whatever you do, whether in word or deed, do it all in the name of the Lord Jesus, giving thanks to God the Father through him.

Our core values are community (Colossians 3:12-15), teaching (verse 16), worship (verse 16), and ministry (verse 17). We believe that community is the primary way people come into relationship with Christ and therefore into God's family. Each week we inquire of first time attendees how they found out about our church. Ninety percent of the people attend because a friend invited them. We're also committed to community groups and events that can give people more opportunities to meet new people and begin to share life with them.

Community is our "front door."

Next, we provide relevant teaching that intends to provide a catalyst for further thought and contemplation. Our senior pastor is committed to beginning his messages with stories, jokes, or some other nonthreatening material so people who have never attended church might feel comfortable. He continues by discussing applicable topics and then follows up by introducing Scripture that addresses those very issues. We encourage everyone to continue learning so that his or her life might be a teaching tool for someone else.

Our third core value is worship. I will describe in detail later how this functions, but our premise is that once we have introduced people to Christ and they begin their relational journey with him, they should come to understand that our very reason for existence is to worship God.

> *Once we have introduced people to Christ and they begin their relational journey with him, they should come to understand that our very reason for existence is to worship God.*

Finally, our fourth core value is ministry. In many churches the members are gathered and even corralled within the walls of the church. Our desire is that people would discover the unique calling that God has placed on their lives and pursue it with passion and integrity. For some, this takes place by serving or leading within the church. For most, however, this takes place by participating in or starting ministries outside of the church. We want to see that people not only learn about Christ and his mission, but that they take an active part in giving back. We want to be active in building God's Kingdom, not "our kingdom."

We have found that having these four core values give our entire church a strategic outlook and purpose for living out the example of Christ. As Gen Xers ministering to Gen Xers, we consider worship a *core value,* not merely a piece of programming or filler. In fact, we consider worship to be as important a step in our spiritual life as any other Christian discipline.

Worship as a Core Value

It's the dawn of the third millennium, and worship has never looked quite like this. Pockets of believers across the world are worshipping God in their own setting and style. For some, that means acoustic guitars and voices; for some, it's drums and pipes; for some it's brass and organs; for some it's visual arts and poetry; for others it's dance and drama. Whatever the approach, people are discovering God and his mighty provision in a hurting world. As humans, we hunger and thirst for something more…something bigger. We want to be inspired. We want to dream. In the midst of our search, God waits patiently with the answers to all of our questions and the resources to fulfill all of our desires.

Worshippers around the world are also becoming unified by a new tide of music being written by dedicated women and men of God from every country and creed. We no longer want to be separated. We long to partner with one another to promote the love of Christ to the world.

Worship is the single most important thing in life. A.W. Tozer writes, "Why did Christ come? Why was He conceived? Why was He born? Why was He crucified? Why did He rise again? Why is He now at the right hand of the Father? The answer to all these questions is, 'In order that He might make worshippers out of rebels; in order that He might restore us again to the place of worship we knew when we were first created.' "[2]

Humanity was born out of God's desire for worship. Worship is the doorway to God's love and provision. When we become worshipful people, the floodgates open and God enters our lives.

It's our desire to learn how to direct our hearts toward God. He created us for his good pleasure, and someday we will enter into a place of eternal worship in his presence. As believers, we have a choice regarding how we live our lives today. Our prayer is that we would continually strive to be worshipful people. Being a worshipful person involves singing praises to him, giving sacrificially of our resources, reading his Word, and communicating our love to God and his people. Being a worshipful person is an attitude of the heart, an ongoing appreciation for God in everything we see or do. Worshipful people find joy in the simple things and are inspired enough to embrace the impossible things. When we have this attitude, God's presence ceases to be an experiential feeling and becomes a reservoir out of which life and love flow. As Brother Lawrence puts it, "I began to live as if there were no one but God and myself in the world."[3] Or as Frederick Buechner describes, "In general rejoice in him and make a fool of yourself for him the way lovers have always made fools of themselves for the one they love."[4]

> *Worshipful people find joy in the simple things and are inspired enough to embrace the impossible things.*

As the worship pastor of The Next Level Church, I've been an observer of some incredible events in the life of Christ's church. When we started TNLC in 1993 as a ministry "to Gen Xers by Gen Xers," I had no idea what God was preparing to do in the area of worship. Since that time, God has written some of the most inspiring stories into people's lives and still continues to amaze me and those in the church on a daily basis.

Our church is a hodgepodge of people of all ages, denominations, backgrounds, and personalities, and yet we seem to come together to worship God in a singular voice. Charismatics, conservatives, traditionalists, and seekers are all here worshipping God as he leads them—not as we prompt them.

As humans, we are natural worshippers. The question isn't, Do we worship? for we all do in one way or another. The question is, Who or what do we worship?" People flock to concerts of their favorite artists. They adorn themselves with the appropriate attire. They give their time and money, sometimes sacrificially, for the opportunity to be with thousands of others who, like them, love the common focus and stake a portion of their lives on it. We know how to worship. We need to learn how to worship *God*.

In the past we have equated the term "worship" with music and the arts. However, worship is so much more than a presentational event. People can worship in many ways—through prayer, sacrifice of time or money, poetry, music, dance, and so on. *Any expression of favor toward God is an act of worship*. The goal then is to live our lives as an act of worship. That means every thought, every action, every attitude, every reaction, every word, every relationship becomes an expression of total homage to the Father, the Son, and the Spirit. When we worship in this way, God meets with us and does things in our midst that he could not any other way.

I hear stories of people who are being emotionally healed through worship. I hear from people who never thought they would raise their hands to God being unable to hold back during worship. I

> *Any expression of favor toward God is an act of worship.*

hear how God is using personal worship times to bring people closer to him. I hear people say that they couldn't get through the week if it weren't for worship. People are learning to rely on God more completely. They're learning to appreciate him for who he is and for all of the phenomenal things he does. People are learning to live worshipful lives. This is only the beginning, but we are finally learning how to fear God.

A Model for Gen-X Worship

Let me describe some components that have worked for me and our church in the area of worship with Generation X. I know better than to think that these ideas will solve any or all of the problems all worship leaders face. These are simply things that have worked for us and may offer some insight into Gen-X worship for other leaders.

Worship as an "Event." Most ministries use some type of "event" as the primary tool for reaching their audience. Our event happens to take place on a Tuesday night. I know it may sound odd, but we have found that having a weekday service allows the people of our church to attend with an amazing amount of freedom and energy. People often need the weekend to do other things like accommodating inflexible job hours or actually taking a Sabbath day's rest.

There are several components that we take into consideration as we plan for our services. First, we consider that many people attending may not have been to church in a long time and may have some lingering pessimism about their last experience. Many in our generation have never attended church at all. As a church that's administrated largely by Gen Xers to Gen Xers, we understand how these people feel because we've been there ourselves. Our staff is composed of people who have varied church backgrounds. When we develop an environment for those attending, we start by considering what *we* would look for in a church experience. So far, the results have been amazing.

Before our service, we have people who greet attendees in the parking lot, the front doors, the foyer, the doors to the auditorium, and inside the auditorium itself. We generally have music playing, along with computer slides that show words of welcome and upcoming events. Our stage is set up in a fashion similar to many concerts: drums on risers, multiple riser levels for instrumentalists and vocalists, and lighting that's produced to flow with the programming. We find this setup creates an environment familiar to my generation; it makes us feel at home.

Worship Leading. I felt called to lead worship in my early teens. I attended many youth camps and retreats where worship through music was a critical component of the camp experience. Since that time I've observed dozens of other worship leaders and their styles with which they lead. I've discovered that for my generation, the narrative-commentary style of worship leading doesn't work well. It's usually more of a distraction than a benefit. Many worship leaders use the worship time as a mini-sermon to relate what they've learned in their walk. Inherently, there's nothing wrong with this as long as the audience is benefiting from the experience. For our Gen-X crowd, however, I've chosen to use words sparingly in order to maintain continuity. As a result, I've had many people commend me for not interrupting the worship time by introducing every song or espousing my own thoughts in every quiet moment.

This mode of operation has aided our team in avoiding the ever-present "performance trap." I agree with Sally Morgenthaler when she states, "I've concluded that the overriding problem was the worship leading, or, more accurately, the worship *performance.*"[5] In addition, our worship team is committed to entering into authentic worship ourselves, which rids us of the temptation to transform worship into a performance. I share the worship leader role with the entire team also in an effort to minimize the perception that it is all about me.

Worship leading is a delicate craft. I continually pray that the worship that I am expecting our crowd to participate in is also an outlet for me to participate as well. When I can stand before them, authentic in my own worship, then the crowd is given the permission to experience worship in their own way as well.

Worship Programming. Our music is a blend of vintage Maranatha and Integrity's Hosanna! Music with a new layer of original music that I've written over the past couple of years. We're in the process of incorporating other music as well, from Delirious?, Maranatha's LateLate Service, and Vineyard Music.

> When I can stand before them, authentic in my own worship, then the crowd is given the permission to experience worship in their own way as well.

There are several things we do when choosing music for worship. We carefully examine the texts of songs we use to make sure that the worship time is understandable and applicable. In my experience many worship songs use vocabulary that can be awkward to the listener. Without reducing the amount of meaning, we try to select material that's simple, but rich in depth. We use language that's conversational. For example, this is an excerpt from a song I wrote that we sing with regularity.

> "For all the times You have rescued me,
> For all the times You had faith in me,
> For all the times You forgave me,
> For all the times You sustained me,
> I am so thankful."[6]

Because Generation X is extremely musically literate, we also pay careful attention to musical arrangements and instrumentation. We hope that people can walk into our worship service without experiencing a sudden time warp into the past. We attempt to keep our sounds similar to the sounds that are current at the time. While our team doesn't change style entirely with each passing musical fad, we do incorporate new arrangements as often as possible.

For example, there was a time when I led worship from the keyboard or piano. A few years ago I realized that in order to keep up with the changing sounds, I needed to transition to a guitar-driven musical identity. Shortly thereafter I began writing new songs from the guitar and practicing for the time when I could lead from the acoustic guitar rather than the keys. It took some time, but God graciously allowed me to pick up enough skill to begin leading with a guitar. Today there are people who never knew that I led from keyboards first.

Transitions and continuity are also vital to me as I program for a given worship service. Time after time I've seen poor transitions break up a beautiful worship moment. It's crucial to maintain a certain level of continuity throughout the worship time. We accomplish this through keeping the lapsed time between songs minimal, using instrumental segues between elements of the service, having different members of the band count off intros so I can change instruments quickly, and programming musical sets so that there is a musical thread that keeps the pace continuous.

Some who hear this may accuse me of "programming God." However, I believe, that as worship leaders it's our responsibility to create a well-crafted environment that allows God to move with the least amount of human distraction. We desire to be "invisible" elements, as it were, in the worship experience. When we prepare ourselves as adequately as possible, we can then step out of the "limelight" and allow God to move in people's lives rather than trying to manipulate their experience.

Worship Production. Production elements have the ability to fashion an incredible experience or destroy a wonderful moment. Without diminishing the power of God, production has more influence over the worship event than any other component. The production elements include audio, video (visuals, slides,

As worship leaders, it's our responsibility to create a well-crafted environment that allows God to move with the least amount of human distraction.

video clips, and live camera), stage lighting, house lighting, staging, and props. Something as simple as turning on a microphone or raising a lighting cue can make or break the continuity of a worship experience. Although I don't ever want to be consumed by the production elements, I'm a firm believer in high-quality production.

Why is production so important? Most of my generation has grown up in an MTV, Nintendo, and now Internet environment. Movies have replaced reading. As a generation we're accustomed to the highest level of production. Millions of dollars are spent while producing a motion picture or even a new music video. It would be a shame for people to attend church only to find that our production level has been left in the '70s while the rest of the world has moved on to new and better ideas.

In many cases production quality isn't a matter of money or equipment. Sometimes we need to stand back objectively and see if there are areas that could be improved by simple measures. Usually there are creative ideas that can be implemented in the areas of lighting and staging, even in the worst of rooms. Use of candles, drapings, backlighting, low-lighting, and ambient pre-music are just a few examples of relatively low-cost production boosters. My main concern is that we should not consider production quality and value lightly. Production is an area that deserves excellence.

Worship Teams. The "team" concept is extremely important to Gen Xers—and that has implications for the way we worship. At my church we actually have two different worship teams. Our primary worship team leads the weekly services and often travels to conferences, retreats, camps, and other events as we are invited. Our second team is the gospel choir. This team rehearses once a month and participates in our service once a month. The gospel choir consists of about thirty members who sing material ranging from traditional black gospel to contemporary pop. This team provides an outlet for a large number of people within the church who have musical ability. We include the same basic components in both of our worship teams:

• Relationships and Camaraderie. At the foundation of either of our worship teams is a value for genuine relationship. Our worship teams function more as a family than as a group of people who happen to play music together. We share life together. We have been to each other's homes. We share prayer requests and commit to pray for each other regularly. We take trips together. We cry together. And we certainly laugh together.

When I interview a potential team member, I might say, "If you join this team, you join a family—not just a band." Typically when someone comes onto the team, we all echo, Welcome to the family! Lately each existing team member has shared with the new members what they should expect as they join our musical family. We've also shared what the team means to us personally, and emphasize the fact that we're all in this together—sink or swim, succeed or fail, in joy and in sorrow.

> *Our worship teams function more as a family than as a group of people who happen to play music together.*

• Rehearsals. Rehearsals are the lifeblood of our team. Each Thursday evening we meet at half past six to review the previous worship time. We discuss observations, thoughts, and feelings that we have or have heard from others about the worship experience. We all appreciate hearing other team member's perspective and input about the service. Around seven, instrumentalists and vocalists separate for a rehearsal hour. We rehearse material for the next week as well as work on new material to be introduced at a later date. Around eight, we join together and rehearse as a full team. Usually we have full sound and monitors so we can practice as if it were a typical service. At nine, we pray together, strike, and go home. Having consistent rehearsals has been the primary tool for learning and growing together.

On a rare occasion, I sense from the team that life has been particularly difficult, and I will either cut rehearsal short or call it off altogether. I've found that being sensitive to the physical and emotional condition of the team cultivates a mutual respect and actually increases the level of dedication.

• Additions and Auditions. When it comes time to add new members to the team, I exercise as much patience as possible. I believe that God can introduce the right people at the right time to our team. If someone desires to join the team, I set up a time to meet casually together and get to know the person. I don't ask potential members to prepare something unless they would like to do so. We discuss background, experience, and time schedule. Generally, I keep the entire team up to date with new auditions so that they are the first to know. It's not uncommon to deliberate for months when considering new members of our worship team. When a person joins the team, it becomes the responsibility of the entire team to take care of the new member.

Worship Staff. The Gen-X "team concept" of worship goes beyond the musicians and singers; it includes worship leaders who may never set foot on the stage. Here's a brief outline of the various roles different people play to make our Gen-X worship successful.

• Worship Pastor

1. Creates the overall program for each worship event or service.

2. Shepherds the worship teams. This responsibility includes promoting spiritual development, musical advancement, and rehearsal preparation for each of the worship team members.

3. Collects or creates worship resources including recordings, study materials, and a music library.

4. Teaches a worship "core curriculum." These classes are used to teach our members about worship as a core value for our church.

• Worship Program Administrator

1. Assists the worship pastor.

2. Serves as production coordinator for all worship-related projects.

3. Serves as band director as needed for rehearsals.

• Production Director

1. Supervises the overall production aesthetic for worship events.

2. Maintains a production staff that handles all production aspects of events and services including sound, lighting, visuals, recording, video coverage, and setup and tear down.

• Worship Vocal Team Manager

1. Serves as vocal director for the worship team and gospel choir.

2. Conducts vocal rehearsals with both teams.

3. Maintains prayer request list for the worship teams.

4. Facilitates spiritual development through study and prayer directly with the vocal team.

The Future of Worship

The eras of change in worship are occurring more rapidly than ever before. There was a time when a worship era could span hundreds of years. Then, in the early 1900s, eras typically changed every ten years or so. In the third millennium, I wouldn't be surprised to see changes happening nearly every year. As a Gen Xer, such rapid change in worship forms and styles is not much of a concern. We are comfortable with change. Authenticity, experience, mystery, relationship, honesty, and truth concern us more.

Ultimately the future may not be an issue of adaptation; it may be more about regeneration. Let me explain what I mean. Many Boomer churches today are trying various approaches to "adapt" their worship services so that they can attract a Gen-X audience. Unfortunately, the results of these efforts often appear superficial or "fake" to people in my generation—like trying to put new wine in old wineskins. Instead of trying to adapt to generational changes on their own, leaders in the new millennium should be looking for ways to *regenerate* their ministries in a new form altogether by investing in young emerging leaders who have the resources needed to lead their churches into the future.

Holistic Worship. Generation X has already come of age and in the not-too-distant future will take the leadership reins of the church. When that happens, it may come as a surprise to discover that our worship time will not look anything like our elders'. The modernist mentality likes things fairly clean-cut, concise, thorough, and not too open to interpretation. Service begins at this time and ends at that time. Not much room for variance. This approach to worship may have served us well in the past, but it can seem stale and forced to people in my generation.

Our elders were raised on radio and television. What they tuned into is what they received. Gen Xers, on the other hand, were raised in a world of fast-paced production, video games, virtual reality, interactive media, and the Internet. If we don't care for what's on TV, we have a thousand other choices. Our worship for the most part has reflected this phenomenon. As we gaze into the future, perhaps our worship services should begin to reflect the interactive nature of the Gen-X and

Millennial environment. I envision a time when our service will be a mixture of multiple elements being presented simultaneously for the congregation. During worship, we might have a band playing; computer-generated slides with texts, Scriptures, and images; video; artwork; drama; dance; and poetry available in printed form or spoken at a time of meditation. From start to finish, an attendee could choose which elements to tune in to and draw from for their edification. Perhaps afterward we would all spend time together listening to more music, sharing stories, writing songs, eating together, serving each other, or praying together. What may sound like a departure is actually an arrival back to the roots of the early church (see Acts 2:42-47 and Colossians 3:12-17).

> *I envision a time when our service will be a mixture of multiple elements being presented simultaneously for the congregation.*

The idea of holistic worship—worship that encompasses intellect, emotions, and physicality—will certainly be a reality in the near future. Gen-X Christians want more than a program or somber sing-along. We want to experience God in an incredible way. We desire to know him intimately and personally. We want to know the deep rich meaning of the things we do and see. We want to want what he wants.

New Songs. Over the past twenty years, hundreds, if not thousands, of songs have been written for the praise and worship genre. For most churches it has been acceptable to play the same songs each week year after year. In the 1990s with bands such as Delirious as well as other music from the United Kingdom, Australia, Africa, and the United States, the styles, sounds, and structures of worship music have changed dramatically. Songs have shifted from ensemble arrangements to band arrangements. There is more utilization of rhythmic sounds and instruments. We have only just begun to see the impact of rhythmic sounds in our worship. From elaborate percussion to electronically generated techno sounds, rhythm will soon have its place at the forefront of worship. We have already incorporated drum solos and techno-soundscape tracks during offering and extensive percussion-groove intros and transitions.

> *We have only just begun to see the impact of rhythmic sounds in our worship.*

I believe the emergence of new material is going to be key to the progress of worship in the future. The songs we sing today will likely have a "shelf life" that is less than half that of the songs written in the '70s and '80s. For example, most worship leaders know "Lord, I Lift Your Name on High," a song that's been dubbed "America's Most Beloved Worship Song." While I appreciate Rick's writing and actually love the song myself, the people in my church refer to it as "an oldie but a goodie." Over the past several years, I've introduced my own original songs to our church. For some, a song written just a few years ago seems dated and antiquated. This tells me that I need to continue writing and producing records so that we will have renewed freshness in our worship together.

Overall, tastes are changing more and more rapidly as the months go by. It's up to the worship leaders to continually introduce new songs to the people. Even the psalms challenge us to "sing to the Lord a new song." God is infinitely creative and he created us in his image. We should feel compelled to share new songs with him and his people. New songs and music will keep the momentum alive into the future.

Resources for Personal Worship. The fact that we should be worshippers in our private lives seems obvious, but for most it's a difficult discipline to develop. Corporate worship experiences are relatively easy to find. There are as many different styles of churches as there are people groups. Worshipping God alone is another matter. When we learn that reading the Word and praying are forms of worship, then it gets a little simpler. But what if a person needs more support or help when it comes to worshipping alone?

Worship records, study materials, videos, devotionals, or any other form of audio or video stimulus can provide the means by which people may worship creatively in their own setting. Many people love to worship in the car. Many people enjoy reading about Scriptures as they relate to their favorite songs. For some, worship videos are a great way to experience the corporate setting without actually being there.

Last year we began building a series of worship projects that are intended to be more than just another worship record with some good songs. The project "ONE" includes a CD with twelve favorite songs from Maranatha, Hosanna's Integrity, Rich Mullins, Russ Taff, and others. "ONE Study," a devotional guide, is also available. The study follows each track on the recording and offers corresponding lyrics, Scriptures, study thoughts, composers' notes, and probing questions for the reader to think about, pray about, and answer. Our second project, "TWO," is also now available. "TWO" is comprised of entirely original music that I have been writing over the past couple of years. This project also has a study guide companion. We intend to continue producing projects of this nature as long as material is available.

A Final Thought

In 1 Peter 2:16-17, Peter writes, "Live as free men, but do not use your freedom as a cover-up for evil; live as servants of God. Show proper respect to everyone: Love the brotherhood of believers, fear God, honor the king." As Christians we enjoy freedom in Christ that compels us to worship him. Our worship should not be self-serving, but selfless. Likewise, our worship should reflect our love for the brotherhood of believers and show proper respect for everyone who worships with us.

Worship has power to completely transform our lives. God desires to connect with us. Worship can help make that happen. I ask that you pray that God would continue to show you and me exactly what he has in mind as we journey into the future. I also ask whatever you do, whether in word or deed, that you will do it in the name and for the sake of the Lord Jesus. And as you do those things, give thanks to God the Father and worship him above all things.

NOTES

1. Tim Celek and Dieter Zander with Patrick Kampert, *Inside the Soul of a New Generation* (Grand Rapids, MI: Zondervan Publishing House, 1996), 26.

2. A.W. Tozer, *Worship: The Missing Jewel of the Evangelical Church* (Harrisburg, PA: Christian Publications, Inc.), 23.

3. Brother Lawrence, *The Practice of the Presence of God* (Springdale, PA: Whitaker House, 1982), 49.

4. Frederick Buechner, *Wishful Thinking: A Seeker's ABC* (New York, NY: HarperCollins Publishers, 1993), 122.

5. Sally Morgenthaler, "Leading vs. Performance," Worship Leader (July/August 1997), 16.

6. From the song "I Am So Thankful," John S. Miller.

Chapter 9

A New Reformation:

Re-Creating Worship for a Postmodern World

by LEONARD SWEET

T he journal Philosophy and Literature, published by the University of Canterbury, in Christchurch, New Zealand, periodically gives Gold Medal awards in the "Bad Writing Contest." One of the recent award winners was the distinguished scholar Fredric Jameson, whose opening sentence in *Signatures of the Visible* (1998) gives a portent of what follows:

> The visual is *essentially* pornographic, which is to say that it has its end in rapt, mindless fascination; thinking about its attributes becomes an attribute to that, if it is unwilling to betray its object; while the most austere films necessarily draw their energy from the attempt to repress their own excess (rather than from the more thankless effort to discipline the viewer).

In close second was a professor of English, Rob Wilson. His "winning" paragraph went like this:

If such a sublime cyborg would insinuate the future as post-Fordist subject, his palpably masochistic locations as ecstatic agent of the sublime superstate need to be decoded as the 'now-all-but-unreadable DNA' of a fast deindustrializing Detroit, just as his Robocop-like strategy of carceral negotiation and street control remains the tirelessly American one of inflicting regeneration through violence upon the racially heteroglossic wilds and others of the inner city.[1]

Easy for him to say. But it is not just academics who are speaking and writing in "secret code" language that reflects their professional class or occupational superiority. From the perspective of "outsiders" in this post-Christian culture, much of mainline Protestantism has been speaking in a foreign language for decades.

In the midst of one of the greatest transitions in the history of Christianity—from modern to postmodern—mainline churches remain stuck in a modern paradigm. They have clung to modern modes of thought and action, their ways of embodying and enacting the Christian tradition frozen in patterns of modernity.

The decline of mainline Christianity is so well-documented it needs no rehearsing here. In fact, the mainline plight has passed into the realm of humor. At a recent board meeting of a community agency, someone used the phrase "mainline churches." Someone else asked, "What are mainline churches?" A third snapped back, "The ones with the fewest people."

For the first time in U.S. American history more people are attending non-denominational than denominationally affiliated churches. In one year alone (1997 to 1998), average church size plummeted over 10 percent, with a drop of 15 percent during the same twelve-month period in annual operating budgets.[2] The fact is that most of the mainline church is in serious deterioration or comatose.

My favorite example of how out of touch mainliners can be with the emerging postmodern world all around them is a throwaway line from Marc Driscoll, Gen-X pastor at Seattle's thriving Mars Hill Fellowship. Driscoll says his challenge in reaching postmoderns is not convincing them that Jesus rose from the dead or that there could be such a thing as a resurrection. His biggest challenge is in convincing postmoderns that there was only one resurrection.

The mainline church went to sleep in a modern world governed by the gods of reason and observation. It is awakening to a postmodern world open to revelation and hungry for experience. Indeed, one of the last places postmoderns expect to be "spiritual" is the church. In the midst of a spiritual heat wave in the host culture, the mainline church is in the midst of a deep freeze.

> *The mainline church went to sleep in a modern world governed by the gods of reason and observation. It is awakening to a postmodern world open to revelation and hungry for experience.*

The mainline crisis is of "EPIC" proportions. It will take more than a Martha Stewart makeover or spiritual plastic surgery to make mainline worship vital to a postmodern culture. Unless mainline churches can transition their worship into more EPIC directions—Experiential, Participatory, Image-Based, and Communal—they stand the real risk of becoming museum churches, nostalgic testimonies to a culture that is no more.

From Rational to Experiential

A modernist dies and finds himself surrounded by dense, billowy clouds which only allow him to see a short distance ahead of him. He sees that he is walking down a road paved in gold. Ahead, there is a slight break in the clouds. He sees a signpost and a fork in the

> "*Sometimes you can-not believe what you see, you have to believe what you feel.*"
> —*Brandeis professor Morrie Schwartz to Mitch Albom in* Tuesdays With Morrie. *³*

road. The signpost has inscriptions with golden arrows pointing to the left and right.

The modernist reads them. The right arrow says, "This way to heaven." The left arrow says, "This way to a discussion about heaven."

Guess which fork the modernist took?

The perpetual openness to experience of postmoderns is such that one can never underestimate the e-factor: experiential.

Welsh priest and poet R.S. Thomas, when out walking in the countryside of Wales, has a custom of putting his hand in the place where a hare has recently lain, hoping to find it still warm. ⁴

Postmoderns are constantly putting their hands and the rest of themselves where God may have visited; hoping it's still warm. They are hungry for experiences, especially experiences of God.

The postmodern economy is an experience-based economy. In my lifetime we have transitioned from an industrial economy (which manufactured widgets) to an information economy (which generated information) to an experience economy (which traffics in experiences). The precise nature of this new economy has been summarized exquisitely by Marilyn Carlson Nelson, the new Chair, President, and CEO of Carlson Companies, one of the world's largest privately held companies:

> Anyone who views a sale as a transaction is going to be toast down the line. Selling is not about peddling a product. It's about wrapping that product in a service—and about selling both the product and the service as an experience. That approach to selling helps create a vital element of the process: a relationship. In a world where things move at hyperspeed, what was relevant yesterday may not be relevant tomorrow. But one thing that endures is a dynamic relationship that is

grounded in an experience that you've provided.[5]

Already U.S. American consumers spend more on entertainment than on health care or clothing.[6] Whatever happened to the fountain pen? Ask Mont Blanc how much high-tech postmoderns want high-touch experiences with their fingers.

REI's flagship store in Seattle looks more like a retail amusement park than a store. One of the country's largest wilderness-sports stores (100,000 square feet; 60,000 stock items), the consumer cooperative Recreational Equipment, Inc. (REI), boasts places for customers to interact with and experience some of the products it sells—a seven-story climbing wall; a 300-foot waterfall; a 475-foot-long biking trail and test track; a one hundred-seat cafe; a rain room for testing how waterproof Leak-Tex is; a lab where camp stoves can be tried out; and so on. The aisles between departments are even designed to resemble hiking trails.

Honda has based an entire sales strategy on an "experiential" foundation. Honda's success with its four hundred supplier companies throughout North America is based on what it calls The Three Joys. According to The Three Joys, each component in the "car experience" (customer, employee, supplier) should enjoy the "experience." Customers should have a positive experience of ownership. The dealer who connects the customer to the supplier should enjoy the experience of bringing pleasure to the customer—high customer satisfaction. Honda, who supplies the product, should enjoy the experience of pleasing both other parties with such a superb product.

> "*Engineering. Science. Technology. All worthless…unless they make you feel something.*"—ad for BMW's 3-Series cars

Why is tourism one of if not *the* fastest growing industry in the world? It creates a new job every 2.5 seconds and generates investments of $3.2 billion *a day*. Almost two trillion dollars is spent annually on tourism worldwide, accounting for one-tenth of the global economic impact. More than 200 million people are employed worldwide by an industry that will grow to 350 million employees by 2005.[7]

Some scholars interpret the touristic phenomenon as a postmodern ritual that performs the same role as sacred rites did in premodern societies. Heritage tourism appeals to a culture's search for "authenticity," "otherness," "identity," and educational experiences while vacationing.

In 1994, 528 million people traveled for the pleasure of experiences of "otherness." By 2010 this figure is expected to rise to 937 million. Half the world's vacationers head to the sea each year—and half the world's people live within fifty miles or so of saltwater. But tourism has reached every region of the globe—from the mountains to the desert, from the polar icecaps to the tropical rain forests. It will soon reach the moon first and then Mars. What will get us there will not be government space agencies, but Hilton and Ritz-Carlton.

Why is travel and tourism the United States' largest export industry as well as our second largest employer (after health) and third largest retail industry (after automotive and food store sales)?

Because tourism is an experience industry. The fastest-growing segment of tourism is adventure travel, with over two hundred travel books appearing each month catered to this clientele. Adventure travel will likely become in our lifetime the largest commercial use of space once reusable launchers reduce costs sufficiently for space tours to orbiting space stations. It is not surprising that in an experience economy frequent mall shopping would plummet, down from 16 percent in 1987 to fewer than 10 percent in 1998. Yet at the same time the Mall of America (Bloomington, Minnesota) now hosts more visitors than Walt Disney World, Disneyland, and the Grand Canyon *combined.*[8] Why? It's not a mall, but an experience center.

Here's the point: *In postmodern culture, the experience is the message.* Postmoderns literally "feel" their way through life. If postmodern worship can't make people furiously *feel* and *think* (in the old "modern" world, we would have said only "think"), it can't show them how God's Word transforms the way we "feel."

Postmodern preachers don't "write sermons"—they create experiences. And these *Shekhinah* experiences (*Shekhinah* is the Hebrew term for the divine presence) bring together all the senses—sound, sight, touch, taste, and smell—into a radiant glowing of God's presence dwelling with God's people suffused in the ethereal light of beauty, truth, and goodness.

> **P**ostmodern preachers don't "write sermons"—they create experiences.

It will not be easy for mainline Protestantism to make this transition to worship that meets the "wow" standard. As much as the modern university, the mainline church is the intellectual outgrowth of the Enlightenment, which tried to make the critical use of reason, not experience, the touchstone of knowledge. Jane Miller recalls her experience at Cambridge in the mid-twentieth century: "I have to admit, I believed you should not include anything you actually thought or felt in an essay."[9]

The triumph of Enlightenment rationalism in worship is demonstrated in the statistics of a 1998 Barna Research Group study, which found that 32 percent of all types of regular churchgoers have never experienced God's presence in worship. Forty-four percent have not experienced God's presence in the past year. And the younger you are, the less likely you are to have a religious experience in worship.

As appalling as these figures are, the percentages would be even higher if mainline Protestants were isolated out for comparison.

At a gathering of seven hundred mainliners, I watched in amazement as the entire congregation obediently followed the instructions in the bulletin, turned to the page for the black spiritual "Amen, Amen" and read from their hymnals, with heads bowed and legs braced, the one-word song: "A-men, a-men, a-men, a-men, a-men." It's definitely time for a change.

From Representative to Participatory

Here's a conversation overheard in a restaurant:

"Give me a Coke."

"Would you like a Classic Coke, a New Coke, a Cherry Coke, or a Diet Coke?"

"I'd like a Diet Coke."

"Would you like a regular Diet Coke or a caffeine-free Diet Coke?"

"The heck with it. Give me a 7UP."

Postmoderns don't give their undivided attention to much of anything without it being interactive.

A choice culture is by definition a participatory culture. Postmoderns don't give their undivided attention to much of anything without it being interactive. In fact, the more digital the culture becomes, the more participatory it gets. The notion that electronic culture produces "couch potatoes" has pockmarked the mind of the church for too long. The truth is just the opposite. The more you surf the Internet, the more you become "surf bored," as Jim L. Wilson puts it,[10] and want to surf the real thing.

This is one reason for the decreasing popularity of television in postmodern culture. The finale of *Seinfeld* attracted 76.3 million viewers in 1998. The finale of *Cheers* attracted 80.5 million viewers in 1993. The finale of *M*A*S*H* attracted 106 million viewers in 1983. That's a drop of 30 million viewers while during the same time the total number of television households grew by 16 million.[11]

Why? Television isn't nearly interactive enough. With a wired universe, each person can be a programmer, not just an observer. Television news has a stable audience only among those fifty or older. Everyone else is getting his or her information elsewhere. No wonder interactivity is the central focus of content providers, with an interactive *Sesame Street* now being prepared that will run on WebTV.

In economics there are fewer "professionals" as more people are becoming their own online stockbrokers and with an astonishing 41 percent of U.S. households having become stockholders.

In religion there are no more "professional clergy" and pew-sitting laity. There are only ministers who look to leaders to mobilize and release ministry through them.

Naturally this shift in culture also applies in worship. Postmoderns want interactive, immersive, in-your-face participation in the mystery of God. That's why they are attracted to the power and mystery of Pentecostalism—which is the fastest growing religious movement in the world.[12] That desire to explore the "mystery" of worship has also drawn postmoderns toward neo-traditional faiths. Sometimes, in fact, the Pentecostals and the neo-traditionalists have actually combined forces. For example, there is a fifteen hundred-seat sanctuary Pentecostal church in Valdosta, Georgia, which converted en masse to the Book of Common Prayer, with a bishop of the Episcopal Church carrying out the confirmation of the entire congregation on Good Friday 1990.

Postmodern worship is body worship. Body piercings show postmodern desperation for rituals, including body rituals. People are narrating the story of their lives on their bodies through multiple piercings (a dozen piercings are not uncommon). The role of spectacle in worship is only beginning to be understood.

Ironically it is the screen that releases postmoderns to "put their whole being" into worship and frees them up from being chained in place by books. Sometimes the preaching will become more karaoke, other times more kinesthetic. But whatever form preaching takes, the interactive component is crucial. Unless postmoderns can complete the sentence for themselves, or at least have the opportunity to hold the mike themselves, worship will insufficiently help them create new realities for their lives.

Faced with a smorgasbord of choices, some people don't select one or the other. They select nothing at all. That's why the neo-traditional movement will become stronger than it is now. But while many couples want traditional weddings with all the trimmings, they want tradition "neo." "Neo" for them means tradition customized and personalized. Even neo-traditionalists make the tradition interactive. If they can't take tradition and run with it down their own path, they won't pick it up.

From Word-Based to Image-Driven

"If you want people to think differently," Buckminster Fuller used to say, "don't tell them how to think, give them a tool." The best tool worship leaders can give people to help them think and live differently is a metaphor or image. Nietzsche was right: "We do not think good metaphors are anything very important, but I think a good metaphor is something even the police should keep an eye on."[13]

To sculpt a metaphor is to transform the world. Metaphor (such as metaphor evangelism or metaphor preaching) is the medium through which postmodern spirituality is created for a variety of reasons.

First, humans think in images, not words. In a visualholic culture like postmodernity it is difficult not to believe that using metaphorical "pictures" would make worship more meaningful. But our "image-driven" lifestyle isn't distinctive to postmodern culture, but to the human mind itself. The human mind is made-up of metaphors. In defining realities, metaphors create realities. Metaphors consist of both thought and action. Metaphors are more than matters of language.

> Metaphor is a matter of conceptual structure. And conceptual structure is not merely a matter of the intellect—it involves all the natural dimensions of our experience, including aspects of our sense experiences: color, shape, texture, sound, and so on. These dimensions structure not only mundane experience but aesthetic experience as well. [14]

That's why the power of liturgy is so immense. The ultimate in power is the ability to order and ordain metaphors.

Postmodern spirituality is image-based for a second reason. Postmodern culture is a double-ring culture, [15] and metaphors are themselves a double ring. Philosopher Max Black calls them "two ideas in one phrase" (for example, "sweet smile" or "sharp tongue"). Part of this double-ring effect comes from the shaping influence of chaos theory and complexity science, which look at the whole—the system—rather than the parts. In searching for similarities, complexity thinking invites metaphorical thinking and linking.

Third, worship is not about style; it's about spirit. If the "spirit" isn't right, presentation means little—no matter how contemporary or high-tech. Ten times zero is still zero. And, if the Spirit is there, presentation also means little—no matter how traditional or bookish.

Linda S. McCoy is pastor of The Garden in Indianapolis, which meets in a Beef and Boards Dinner Theater facility. The musical group The Good Earth Band leads worshippers seated around tables through heavy helpings of video clips, drama, secular music, and contemporary Christian music—keeping the service to a thrifty forty minutes. A flowerpot container at the door is the only offering plate.

The importance of shifting worship from the exegesis of words to the exegesis of images in the postmodern world was hammered home from studies of companies in *Built to Last* (1996). Two Stanford Business School professors discovered to their surprise that the key to great companies is not "visionary leadership" by some entrepreneurial CEO, but the creation of a network of shared meaning and values around common metaphors that abide and guide the company into the future.[16]

From Individual to Communal

Why is Times Square the most popular place to greet the new millennium? Why are coffee bars the new dating places? Why is the Internet becoming less an information medium than a social medium, with more and more people logging on, not to gain information but to hear "You've Got Mail" and even to find love online?

Relationship issues stand at the heart of postmodern culture. In classic double-ring fashion, the more digitally enhanced the culture becomes, the more we are drawn to flesh-and-blood interaction.

At the heart of postmodernity lies a theological dyslexia: Call it "me/we," or the experience of individual-in-community. Think back on the flowers that were strewn on the sidewalks as part of Princess Diana's funeral. Something registered in your subconscious about those mounds of flowers, even if you didn't call it to rational or verbal consciousness. What was unique about those flowers?

In the medieval world, where everything was communal and

nothing was individual, grieving villagers would have been content to simply pile flowers on top of other flowers. In the modern world, where everything was individual and little was communal, we arranged single bouquets of flowers in individual vases and put them on the altar or grave. In postmodern culture, we put our flowers back on the communal pile, but wrap them in cellophane or plastic to separate them from the crowd. A postmodern "me" needs "we" to "be."

Electronic culture necessitates longer pastoral tenures, not shorter. Building relationships of trust and intimacy in a post-Christian culture takes time. The transient nature of the culture requires that our community-building and hospitality be more aggressive, not less—more premeditated, not haphazard. Dietrich Bonhoeffer's conviction that an anti-Christian culture can actually work for the good of Christianity presupposes a vibrant communal life where people of faith can teach each other to live by faith—which is what God intended in the first place.

The future promises a second coming of communal customs and values. Postmoderns are disillusioned with the hyper-individualism of modern society. In the words of Gen Xer Tom Beaudoin, "My generation inherited not free love but AIDS, not peace but nuclear anxiety, not cheap communal lifestyles but crushing costs of living, not free teach-ins but colleges priced for aristocracy."[17]

Part of this quest for community and communal dimensions of life appear retro and neo-traditional: white wedding gowns, dance halls (swing dancing, ballroom dancing), even church fellowship halls. But the individual quest for communal rituals runs deep. To address this hunger for community, vital worship will need to upgrade four elements. First, three-quarters of all pastors see themselves as gifted either at teaching or preaching.[18] Yet Jesus' ministry had three components: preaching, teaching, and healing. If moral and spiritual transformation is to occur communally as well as individually, pastors will need to upgrade their healing role and hone their healing skills to at least the same levels as preaching and teaching.

Second, like everything else in postmodern culture, worship needs to be decentralized. Postmodern culture brings in its wake a double edge toward global hypercentralization and local decentralization. The one big refrigerator has been replaced by refrigerators you can find in places other than kitchens—bedrooms, family room bars, playrooms, grill areas, custom installed in every cabinet or drawer. Already the California Legislature has considered two proposals to divide California into two new states. Already some twenty-five counties have voted to secede from California.

Worship must become a key component to every small, separate cell group that is free to worship in its own way while integrated into the larger church. Eighty-five percent of churches now offer cell group opportunities, each one of which should include a worship component.

Third, storytelling creates community. The narrative quality of experience is a deeply religious issue. We organize our experience through narrative. We inhabit a storied reality.[19] The modern world exalted abstract principles over "stories." In fact, the poet John Betjeman defined an intellectual as simply a nonvisual person.[20]

The very word "abstract" comes from the Greek *ab*, which means "to move away from," and *strahere,* which means "to stand." To have an abstract relationship with something, one has to stand away from it. To tell a story, one has to step into it and hold it tightly. In fact, according to New Testament scholar Tom Boomershine, "To say 'Let me tell you a story' is like saying, 'Let's go play.' "[21]

The gospel has lost its original character as a living storytelling tradition of messengers who told the good news of the victory of Jesus...telling stories is foreign to contemporary experience. We continue to read Bible stories to children. But the assumption is that once you grow up and learn to think you will stop telling stories and start telling the truth. Telling the truth means you will speak in conceptual abstractions.[22]

Telling stories in a digital culture may take any number of forms in worship: oral, audio, video, television, films, multimedia, and CD-ROM.

Fourth, postmoderns need active worship that leads to service and social transformation. In the words of history of religions scholar Huston Smith, "The heart of religion is not altered states but altered traits of character. For me, then, the test of a substance's religious worth or validity is not what kind of far-out experience it can produce, but is the life improved by its use?"[23]

Forget an annual Mission Sunday. Make every day a mission day and every worship service a mission service. In fact, worship services need to be precisely what they say they are: worship service.

Worship and the "New" Way of Thinking

Modern worship has been trapped in foundationalist thinking where the divine is "out there" to be hauled in by objective methods. EPIC worship will need to evolve in concert with three forces of thought and culture, all of which are creating what is known as a "postmodern." These three forces are (1) postmodern hermeneutics, (2) the hard sciences themselves, and (3) cognition research.

Mainline Protestantism's predominant model of sit-and-soak worship cannot hold up under postmodern hermeneutics and philosophy. It's helpful to remember that just as the Protestant Reformation was a worship revolution wrought by changes in hermeneutics and epistemology, so the current Postmodern Reformation is witnessing revolutions in worship styles and functions wrought by similar forces.

Postmodern Hermeneutics. Why has "praise" music had such a hard time of it in mainline circles? Partly because the modern age was temperamentally allergic to praise. The scientific method was a "critical" method, and moderns were trained to critique, not to cheerlead—to assess, not to applaud.

The postmodern hermeneutics of learning through "interactive observation" are dethroning the old epistemological beliefs that pure learning comes via an under-glass analysis of cold logic, hard facts, and critical distance from the "object" of knowledge. Postmodern theorists are charting the course to a new "scientific method," one whose modes of knowledge are more relational, more experiential, more image-based, and more celebratory and communal.

Unlike their cerebral predecessors, postmodernists believe there are multiple ways of seeing the world. For example, there is more than a single way of "knowing" a flower. One way (more Western) of "knowing" a flower is to be full of oneself, one's wits and wisdom, and to throw oneself against the flower as an object. The other way (more Eastern) of "knowing" is really a way of "unknowing": to be "empty" of oneself and to let the flower reveal itself as it is. The first way of "knowing" a flower is to experiment with it as something separate, to stand at a distance from it, and pick it apart. The second way of knowing a flower is to experience it, to enter in rather than stand back; to stand under (there is no ultimate understanding without standing under) and participate in its beauty.

Knowledge by dissection analytically takes apart; knowledge by dance synthetically puts together. In one you are rich—full of yourself. In one you are poor—empty of yourself. In one you are a distant observer or critic. In one you are an intimate lover.

For the postmodern worshipper, objectivity can no longer be the sole objective of the pursuit of truth. Love can be as much a mode of knowledge as the old scientific method's detachment. Thus a worshipper is both active and reflective, participating and observing, both in and out of the experience.

Hard Sciences. The second influence turning the church toward an EPIC methodology is the "hard" sciences themselves. Chilean immunologist/biologist turned neuroscientist Francisco Varela once remarked that the "hard" sciences deal with the "soft" questions, and the "soft" sciences deal with the "hard" questions. But one of the hardest issues of life is the nature of truth, and here science itself is leading the way in pioneering a new "scientific method" and showing how the old "objective" pursuit of truth is not intellectually sound. The implications of this "new scientific method" for the worshipper are monumental.

> *We do not see things as they are but as we are.—Jewish proverb*

Let me give a smattering of examples to explain what I mean. Particle physicist Edwin Schrödinger states the new paradigm eloquently: The world has not been given to us twice—once in spiritual or psychological terms and once in material terms. The world has been given once. The distinction between subjectivity and objectivity has been useful, but specious.

When Thomas Kuhn wrote his classic text on the *Structure of Scientific Revolutions,* he was only embellishing what Albert Einstein and Karl Popper, in their ruminations on the course of scientific discovery, had already taught us. Both stressed that science advances not through the logic of induction or deduction but through imaginative leaps of faith.[24] A "paradigm shift" is an act of faith which creates new facts and new realities.

In this new approach to science, value and faith commitments become rational parts of a scholar's search for truth. Lorraine Code puts it this way: "Subjectivity—however conflicted and multiple—becomes part of the conditions that make knowledge possible."[25]

Physicist Fred Alan Wolf also lent his support to this new view of reality when he boiled quantum physics down to this statement: "The universe does not exist independent of the thought of the observer" and "You will see it when you believe it."[26] Physicist John Wheeler has advised his colleagues to "cross out that old word 'observer' and replace it by the new word 'participator.' "[27]

Of course, the old scientific method still has its defenders. But one of the untold stories of our time is the movement of the scientific community beyond the modern scientific method. One can see it manifested in British science writer Bryan Appleyard's protestations about "the appalling spiritual damage that science has done" by ignoring questions of meaning and purpose.[28] Or scientist Donald A. Norman's laments over the spiritual and moral vacuum in which much of science is conducted.[29]

Cognition Theories: The third set of influences pushing the church in EPIC directions is the postmodern critique of the modern mindset and especially the emergence of "cognitive sciences." The field of cognition, which includes multiple academic disciplines of neuroscience, psychology, linguistics, genetics, computer science (especially artificial intelligence), anthropology, and philosophy, is generating new insights almost faster than they can be written down.

While some theologians whimper over the loss of modernity's fixed foundations and grounded reference points, scholars such as Humberto Maturana, Gregory Bateson, Heinz von Foerster, George Lakoff, Zenon W. Pylyshyn, Francisco Varela, Eleanor Rosch, and Michael Polanyi are showing how to live and move in an interdependent, relational mindset. Their work is shifting our perspectives from control to flow, from abstract and disembodied reason to embodied and imaginative reason, from representation to participation, from literalism to metaphor.[30]

Barbara McClintock, a geneticist who won the Nobel Prize in 1983 for her lifetime work on the genetics of corn, dissented from modern ways of knowing and suspended the boundaries between subject and object. She developed "a feeling for the organism," and told her biographer Evelyn Fox Keller that things are "much more marvelous than the scientific method allows us to conceive."[31]

The work in the biology of cognition done by Humberto R. Maturana and Francisco J. Varela has shown that cognition is not a representation of the world out there but "an ongoing bringing forth of a world through the process of living itself."[32]

> *You only see what you know.*
>
> *—African proverb*

In many Mediterranean cultures, beauty is more than an intellectual aesthetic. It is an aesthetic of experience, participation, images, and communal celebration. The French scholar Pierre Babin tells of seeing a number of elders sitting motionless under a tree, staring at a picturesque mountain range. He commented to the elders, "Beautiful, isn't it?" They responded, "We feel good here." Babin, unsure whether they understood him properly, tried again. "Your village is so beautiful!" Once more they replied, "Do you feel good in our village?" For them beauty was not fullness of artistry or perfection of lines. It was fullness of being and perfection of presence.

EPIC worship does not give up critical methods of understanding, but rather places them within a larger context of personal reality and experience. And while a worship methodology that is more Experiential, Participative, Imaged-based, and Communal may be classified as "postmodern," it's really nothing new. For Jesus, truth was not a matter of distant observations or scientifically tested theories. Rather, truth was revealed through our participation and interaction with him, others, and the world around us. The same approach rings true for worshippers in a postmodern age.

Notes

1. Rob Wilson, "Cyborg America: Policing the Social Sublime in Robocop and Robocop 2," in *The Administration of Aesthetics: Censorship, Political Criticism, and the Public Sphere,* edited by Richard Burt (Minneapolis: University of Minnesota Press, 1994), 290.

2. George Barna, "Teenagers and Their Relationships," The Barna Report (January-March 1999), 2.

3. *Tuesdays With Morrie: An Old Man, a Young Man, and Life's Great Lesson* (New York, NY: Doubleday, 1997), 61.

4. Elaine Shepherd, *R.S. Thomas: Conceding an Absence* (New York, NY: St. Martin's Press, 1996), 155.

5. As quoted in Fast Company, (November 1998), 108.

6. Michael J. Wolf, "The Pleasure Binge," Wired (March 1999), 86.

7. Spent annually on tourism worldwide: $1.9 trillion. See Peter Weber, "It Comes Down to the Coasts," World Watch (March/April 1994), 21.

8. Wolf, "The Pleasure Binge," Wired (March 1999), 89.

9. Jane Miller, *Seductions: Studies in Reading and Culture* (Cambridge, MA: Harvard University Press, 1991), 151.

10. Southern Baptist pastor Jim L. Wilson uses this phrase in his as yet unpublished article on the "cyber-pastor."

11. Wolf, "The Pleasure Binge," Wired (March 1999), 90.

12. Pentecostalism boasts about twenty million new members a year, with especially large gains in Asia and Africa. Some Latin American countries are approaching Pentecostal majorities. Theologian Harvey Cox wrote his study of Pentecostalism not as an objective observer but as a participant. See Harvey Cox, *Fire From Heaven: The Rise of Pentecostal Spirituality and the Reshaping of Religion in the Twenty-First Century* (Reading, MA: Addison-Wesley, 1995).

13. As quoted by D.J. Enright, *Interplay: A Kind of Commonplace Book* (Oxford: Oxford Press, 1995), 152.

14. George Lakoff and Mark Johnson, *Metaphors We Live By* (Chicago, IL: University of Chicago Press, 1980), 236-237.

15. For more on this, see my "Can You Hear the Double Ring?" Vital Ministry, 2 (March/April 1999), 34-37.

16. James C. Collins and Jerry I. Porras, *Built to Last: Successful Habits of Visionary Companies* (New York, NY: Harper Business, 1994), 212-218.

17. Tom Beaudoin, *Virtual Faith: The Irreverent Spiritual Quest of Generation X* (San Francisco, CA: Jossey-Bass, 1998), 78.

18. George Barna, "Teenagers and Their Relationships," The Barna Report (January-March 1999), 3.

19. Stephen Crites, "The Narrative Quality of Experience," The Journal of the American Academy of Religion, 39 (September 1971), 291-311.

20. As quoted in Mark Amory, "Elegy and Regret." Review of John Betjeman, *Coming Home: An Anthology of His Prose, 1920-1977* (London: Methuen, 1997). Times Literary Supplement (November 12, 1997), 9.

21. Thomas E. Boomershine, *Story Journey* (Nashville, TN: Abingdon, 1988), 18.

22. Boomershine, *Story Journey*, 17.

23. Huston Smith in Marilyn Snell, "The World of Religion According to Huston Smith," Mother Jones (November/December 1997), 43.

24. Karl Popper, *The Logic of Scientific Discovery* (New York, NY: BasicBooks, 1961), 458.

25. Lorraine Code, "Who Cares? The Poverty of Objectivism for a Moral Epistemology," in "Rethinking Objectivity II," edited by Allan Megill, Annals of Scholarship 9:1-2 (1992), 7.

26. Fred Alan Wolf, *Taking the Quantum Leap: The New Physics for Non Scientists* (San Francisco, CA: Harper and Row, 1981) and *Parallel Universes: The Search for Other Worlds* (New York, NY: Simon and Schuster, 1988). See also David Bohm, "Imagination, Fancy, Insight and Reason in the Process of Thought" in *Evolution of Consciousness: Studies in Polarity,* edited by Shirley Sugerman (Middletown, CT: Wesleyan University Press, 1976), 51-68.

27. John Wheeler, "The Universe as Home for Man," American Scientist, 62 (November 1974), 689.

28. Bryan Appleyard, *Understanding the Present: Science and the Soul of Modern Man* (New York, NY: Doubleday, 1992), xvi.

29. Donald A. Norman, *Things That Make Us Smart: Defending Human Attributes in the Age of the Machine* (Reading, MA: Addison-Wesley Publishing Co., 1993), 250.

30. See Rodney Brooks, *Intelligence Without Reason* (Cambridge, MA: Massachusetts Institute of Technology Artificial Intelligence Laboratory, 1991). In Francisco J. Varela's words, "I am claiming that information—together with all of its closely related notions—has to be reinterpreted as codependent or constructive, in contradistinction to representational or instructive. This means, in other words, a shift from questions about semantic correspondence to questions about structural patterns." See his *Principles of Biological Autonomy* (New York, NY: North Holland, 1979), xv. Neni Panourgia's *Fragments of Death, Fables of Identity: An Athenian Anthropography* (Madison, WI: University of Wisconsin Press, 1996) pioneers a new kind of anthropologist, the "communicative agent," which takes participant observation to the highest level and farthest limits.

31. Evelyn Fox Keller, *A Feeling for the Organism: The Life and Work of Barbara McClintock* (New York, NY: W.H. Freeman, 1983), 203.

32. Humberto R. Maturana and Francisco J. Varela, *The Tree of Knowledge: The Biological Roots of Human Understanding* (Boston, MA: New Science Library, 1987), 9, 23.

Group Publishing, Inc.
Attention: Product Development
P.O. Box 481
Loveland, CO 80539
Fax: (970) 679-4370

Evaluation for
Experience God in Worship

Please help Group Publishing, Inc. continue to provide innovative and useful resources for ministry. Please take a moment to fill out this evaluation and mail or fax it to us. Thanks!

• • •

1. As a whole, this book has been (circle one)

not very helpful   very helpful

1	2	3	4	5	6	7	8	9	10

2. The best things about this book:

3. Ways this book could be improved:

4. Things I will change because of this book:

5. Other books I'd like to see Group publish in the future:

6. Would you be interested in field-testing future Group products and giving us your feedback? If so, please fill in the information below:

Name_____

Church Name _____

Denomination _____ Church Size _____

Church Address _____

City _____ State_____ ZIP _____

Church Phone _____

E-mail _____